GIANTS

First published in India by HarperCollins *Publishers* 2025
Cyber City, Building 10-A, Gurugram, Haryana-122002, India
www.harpercollins.co.in

2 4 6 8 10 9 7 5 3 1

Copyright © Huthuka Sumi 2025

P-ISBN: 978-93-6989-591-5
E-ISBN: 978-93-6989-931-9

Huthuka Sumi asserts the moral right
to be identified as the author of this work.

This is a work of fiction and all characters and incidents described
in this book are the product of the author's imagination.
Any resemblance to actual persons, living or dead, is entirely coincidental.

All rights reserved. No part of this publication may be reproduced, stored in
a retrieval system, or transmitted, in any form or by any means, electronic,
mechanical, photocopying, recording or otherwise, without the prior permission of
the publishers.

Without limiting the exclusive rights of any author, contributor or the publisher
of this publication, any unauthorized use of this publication to train generative
artificial intelligence (AI) technologies is expressly prohibited. HarperCollins also
exercise their rights under Article 4(3) of the Digital Single Market Directive
2019/790 and expressly reserve this publication from the text and data-mining
exception.

Typeset in 11.5/16.2 Adobe Caslon Pro at
HarperCollins *Publishers* India

Printed and bound at
Replika Press Pvt. Ltd.

This book is produced from independently certified FSC® paper to ensure
responsible forest management.

HarperCollins *Publishers*, Macken House, 39/40 Mayor Street Upper, Dublin 1,
D01 C9W8, Ireland

GIANTS

HUTHUKA SUMI

Illustrations by Canato Jimo

HarperCollins *Publishers* India

For Levi Kuhu Chishi, firstborn.

For the Nagas, beyond borders.

Contents

Prologue vii

1: Susurration 1

2: Lusaqhi: Pre-planting Month—March 10

3: The Beginning 18

4: Afterglow 33

5: Ipuza—Grandmother 42

6: Mozaqhi: Weeding Month—May 52

7: Amuhaqhi—June 66

8: Aniqhi—July 76

9: The Hunt 87

10: The Reckoning 98

11: The Tail End of a Betrayal 105

Contents

12: A Storyteller?	115
13: Two Tales by Flowing Waters	124
14: Weavings	133
Two Months Later	140
15: A Curio	141
16: Premonitions	149
17: Ghileqhi: Winter's Wind—October	158
18: The Bargain	170
19: Suphuqhi: February	184
20: Ghixuqhi: Planting Season—April	190
21: The Ghost That Everyone Forgot About	199
22: The Last Reckoning	208
23: The Debt	219
24: Aniqhi Once More	232
Epilogue	239

Prologue

It was a strange time, a time when the new hadn't quite replaced the old, yet the old was no longer itself either. Change had struck like lightning but the resilience of the old made its vestiges cling doggedly to the land like fat at the bottom of a cherished cooking pot.

The old songs were still sung, the old dances celebrated, and the old tongues spoken; even the air had a whiff of the yesteryears. Yet, the sharp smell of something else, something new, had begun to assert itself. 'It isn't like the old days,' the older folks said, and though the young folk knew not of these old days they spoke of, even they could sense that something was on the loose. Why, you could almost spot its tail if you looked hard enough.

1

Susurration

Kato shot the flat pebble over the small lake's placid surface, causing a ripple to streak across it like the Thalaxu's web. Lakhi, kini, kuthu, bidi, pungu, tsugho… he counted to six before the stone finally disappeared into the water with a satisfying *plop*! Chuckling to himself, he bent to retrieve another missile from the teetering heap at his feet.

'Oizao! Dear mother! What are you still doing here, you rascal!' A very annoyed voice thundered into his solitude.

He picked up his satchel and watched his mother storm towards him, cane basket swinging from her back. 'Get going this instant or I shall whip the skin off your buttocks!'

Stooping, he picked up one last stone, this one as black as his mother's hearth, and whiffed it onto the water before running away, shooting a defiant look at his tormentor.

If he'd stayed to count, he'd have noticed that the stone skipped over the water thrice before it vanished above the lake. The spot where it disappeared mid-air shifted like the air sometimes does on a really, really hot day—one moment it was there and the next, it simply winked out of sight. But Kato was already racing up the slope, and whatever game was afoot hung in his absence like an unfinished poem. Maybe this game would have an ending, maybe it was never meant to be. For now all Kato cared about was getting as far away from his irate mother as possible.

―

The mountainside was awash with a fiery blush. In the span of a few hundred steps the concentrated redness quickly dissipated into the gradients of the spectrum until it settled on light orange. In this moment, the village looked like a place halfway between the dreams and the waking world. Kato climbed a small boulder for a better view. He closed his eyes, inhaled the sharpness of the cold mountain air, and hopped off with a satisfied smile.

Baring his canines like a fox in hot pursuit, he raced up the steep incline effortlessly, carried on by his windswept feet. Kato sometimes thought that his mother had snatched him from the air, as he, a wind spirit, blew over her garden. He'd always been fast. So very fast! He continued to role-play the fantasy of a snatched wind spirit until his eyes glanced down at his old half-pant fluttering around his thighs like a harassed flag. He laughed aloud and slowed his pace into an easy walk.

Somehow, he doubted that a Sumi wind spirit would ever consent to wear a half-pant, no matter how reduced its station was. He knew that his father had worn nothing but a woven kilt when he was a boy his age, but then the white man had come and told them that they were indecent and needed covering. Now, only old Futhena—the harrier of children, enemy of all that is joyful—still stubbornly wore the kilt in the whole village.

The white men mostly left them alone but even Kato could sense that with their arrival the mountains had taken note and turned sideways like someone trapped in an uneasy dream. These people had brought more than half-pants and funny-looking hats to his mountains. The first time he'd seen one of the English guns at work he'd been both fascinated and terrified in equal measures. There'd been a deafening roar and the great melon perched on a rock had been blown into smithereens within a blink. The memory still filled him with a prickly feeling.

He slowed down his steps to a dragging gait when he saw the empty ground in front of the schoolhouse. He was late and classes had already begun. He fought the urge to turn back the way he'd come.

The school, a single-thatch house with one big room, stood like a jovial, portly old man in the northern end of the village. Just above and behind it stood the grand council hall where all important matters were discussed. The village—Ayito-phu—was located on the top western flanks of a mountain, a strategic choice that had made it virtually unassailable during the old days of headhunting. If one were to be completely factual, the days of headhunting were neither old nor gone, for in the areas that bordered Burma there were still tribes who took great delight in lopping off heads and stacking skulls like the macabre hoard of some unknown devil.

From a distance he could already hear the children roaring raucously as the teacher tried in vain to quiet them down. Children who had previously accompanied their parents to the jhum fields or made mischief all over the village now had to discipline themselves into sitting in the same place for hours—a thing the students hadn't quite learned to tackle. After all, the school was hardly more than a year old.

Just outside the doorway he paused for a moment and regarded the hornet's nest inside. He felt his strength waver. The thought of all the eyes inside, the minds he couldn't read, the faces that could be hiding disgust or worse yet, pity... He drew in a shaky breath and cursed himself for being late. Exhaling slowly he pushed a foot into the dimness of the classroom.

Like a waning storm the uproar settled into a murmur. Aghoto, the only teacher in the school, motioned him inside. Catching sight of his friend Apu, he quickly walked over to him, the back of his neck burning from the eyes boring into him. The scrawny boy pulled him down onto the bamboo bench hard.

'Kato, you are late,' the teacher stated flatly, almost as if he was making an observation about the weather. Kato in turn nodded and looked down at his dusty bare feet. The teacher sighed in resignation before turning his attention back to the class.

The class let out a collective sigh of relief. Kato was a mute, so it wasn't the silence itself that unnerved the children; they'd never heard him make a sound, except for the odd *huh*, or *mmmh*. He'd never made a scene but even the very minuscule possibility of some unexpected reaction, the most unlikely chance that he might respond somehow, built itself into a tension until it was diffused.

'Okay, let's get back to the lesson then,' the teacher said. Some children restarted their tittering and hush-hush sniggering. Kato continued to look at his dusty feet as he felt his ears blush fiercely like the early morning sun.

'Say it once again, Khuzheli,' the teacher ordered a girl, pointing with his stick at some letters on the blackboard.

'C...c...c...catuh,' the girl replied in a terrified voice. Like a cough that had been held in for too long the class spilled forth once more into a torrent of hilarity that caught the teacher up as well, carrying them all away in a joy that sounded like madness. Kato hesitantly joined in with a smile, relieved and thankful that the attention had shifted away from him.

After their classes, which lasted only two hours, Kato and Apu stole some time to climb the big tree outside the school before the teacher chased them away, shaking his head in exasperation, muttering something about naughty boys and their poor parents.

Apu talked enough for the both of them; Kato, as usual, simply grinned at his friend's tall stories. Everyone knew that Apu's incredible stories were mostly made up, but he liked listening to the thin boy and watching his exaggerated gestures and thigh-slapping laughter.

Today his story was about the time his uncle saw a timi-ala, a giant of the forest, while on one of his solitary hunts. 'He said it was taller than two men and had thighs the size of a tree trunk!'

Kato glanced at Apu sideways and chortled under his breath. The imp was up on tiptoes, chest puffed up and arms stretched out—no doubt a very convincing impression of a giant in his mind!

This was how his stories usually went. At first it would start with an uncle, a brother, his father, or an aunt having the most wondrous experience, but soon he would be telling it as if he had been there himself the whole time. Kato never pointed it out; he loved his thin, small friend very much.

'And then it looked right at him! Can you believe that? It looked straight at him!' And so on and so forth it went.

Kato dropped his satchel off at home and, after a quick drink of water, hurried to his parents in the fields beyond the village gates.

He skipped, ran and hopped, stopping for a while to pester a squirrel. His unique gurgling laughter echoed off the huge rock slabs on the wayside when it finally darted into the tall bamboos.

As he crested the small shoulder before his parent's field he could hear their pentatonic singing: his mother's voice high-pitched and wafting, his father's following beneath in a low bass. *Hoi, hoi, hoi…* They used bamboo hoes to work between the taro plants beside the rice. He yelled his funny yell, not self-conscious anymore, and his mother rose from her work to look up as he careened wildly down the small path, always one little misstep away from turning into a dung beetle. She lifted a hand to shade her eyes from the bright sun that hung overhead in the sky, smiling at her little man who filled up her heart so. It was always like this. He wished it would always be like this.

This image of his mother outlined against the terraced fields, one hand raised to her eyes, another resting on the handle of her hoe, would be imprinted in his mind and years later when he thought of her, this was the memory that first sprang into his mind.

His father gave him a disapproving look when he nearly knocked her basket down in his mad run.

Kato's father was older than his mother by nearly two decades, and while she was still full of vital energy, he was beginning to look like an old man. 'When will you grow up, my son?' He sighed resignedly as Kato began to rummage in her basket, looking for something to eat. Finding cooked tapioca inside one of the many leaf-wrapped packets he exclaimed with joy and began to chomp on it with a content look on his face.

'When I'm gone someday you will have to look after your mother. But look at you! Almost a grown man at thirteen and yet…' Kato's father's voice deflated.

His mother laughed gently and tousled Kato's sun-browned hair.

Kato groaned in satisfaction after the midday meal and stretched his body out like a cat on the bamboo mat of the aliha, the little stilted hut that was both a resting place and a temporary storage house in the fields. It was barely big enough for the three of them. His father whittled at a stout length of bamboo that would become the handle of a dao, a machete-like cutting tool, when finished. His mother sat leaning on the doorframe, fanning herself with a thick leaf.

Kato reached out and pulled at her wraparound hekimini. She looked at him without moving her head from the doorframe. The cool breeze would dry out the sweat on her face, leaving behind salt-streaked hair that stubbornly clung to her high well-defined cheekbones and fine jawline. He put his forefinger and index finger on his lips and grunted in their shared sign for stories.

'But you already know all my stories!' she said, feigning a confused look. He shook his head and continued grunting while holding his fingers against his lips.

'Fine, fine…' she said. 'Which one would you like to hear then? How about the story of Anishe?'

Kato shook his head and reached up towards the thatch roof.

'Ah!' She nodded with a mischievous grin. 'You want to hear about Alhou and how he created the world!'

'Mmmmmhhhhh!' He shook his head vigorously and stretched his arms as high as they would go. Driven to frustration by her continued, very poorly acted ignorance, he jumped up, stretching himself on his toes. Thumping around he looked first this way and then another way with what he obviously thought was a fierce scowl.

'What could my little man be on about I wonder…' she said, squinting up at him, the most devious smile hidden behind the innocent look. Kato groaned before thrusting his left hand inches from her face, palm facing upwards. With unmistakable emphasis he thwacked it loudly with his right palm. It was an action he performed whenever he was extremely annoyed or angry. He'd hoped to startle her but she laughed instead.

'He wants to hear the story of the timi-ala.' His exasperated father finally looked up from his whittling. Although he'd never admit it, Kato's father also loved hearing his wife tell her stories. Kato nodded in approval and plopped down. His mother clapped her hands merrily.

She pulled her hekimini around her knees and closed her eyes, her face slipping into a look of concentration and detachment. It was as if behind her closed eyes she had opened a door and stepped into another world, one that was immeasurably more fascinating.

'Listen well, my son,' her voice wafted into his ears like the sound of corn stalks rustling in the breeze.

'There was Alhou, the creator who'd existed since the beginning. He made man and the spirits, the animals, the trees and the plants, the rivers and the mountains. But before he made men, he said to himself, "Man will be weak—fragile as a dead leaf and as foolish as a newly hatched chick. On his own he will not survive this place I've created." So, he decided to make other beings before man, wiser, stronger and much longer-lived. The shi-kheu to look after the animals in the forest, the aki-ghau to look after the homes of men, the aghoki-ghau to look after the rivers and fishes, and finally a giant named timi-ala to look after man's welfare when he wandered the great forests and jungles.'

Kato clapped his hands and oohed. His mother gave him a wry, knowing look. 'One day you will meet the timi-ala and he'll take you with him,' she said in a foreboding voice. Kato looked very pleased at this prospect.

'But these beings,' she continued, 'though created by Alhou to protect and guide men, were capricious and fickle. If you made obeisance to them in the proper way they were at least, if nothing else, indifferent. But if you crossed them, terrible things would happen to you.'

Here, Kato's father, who'd continued whittling at the dao handle, laid it aside and stood up, making the woven bamboo floor creak in protest.

'Kato, your mother will finish the story later.' The tone of his voice was firm and brooked no room for arguments. Kato nodded and stood up to go outside. There was work to be done.

Their tired figures plodded up the steep inclines. His father walked in front with his dao and his mother followed with her basket hanging from around her neck. Kato completed their trio at the back with a bamboo hoe resting on one tired shoulder. He could easily overtake his mother but that wouldn't be the done thing at all. He was her protector after all.

The sun at their back was now a reddish blur almost past the distant peaks. All around the crickets made their insistent chattering, and the wind whispered, rustled and groaned as it wound itself around the thick firs and bamboos.

Along the way they met other villagers heading home from their fields, everyone too tired to manage anything more than a *hoi* and a wave. There were kitchen fires to be kindled and dishes to put on hearths, and no one seemed inclined to stop and chat. No, that was reserved for the night gatherings around the communal village fires, where fantastic tales would be told, and young girls and boys would see monsters and tigers within the orange tendrils reaching greedily towards heaven.

2

Lusaqhi: Pre-planting Month

MARCH

Kato awoke with a start to the sound of his mother's soft singing. Quickly sitting up he scanned his surroundings. The familiar thatch stared back at him, the lone stool his only piece of furniture, his collection of pebbles on the wooden beam. He fell back on his bed, letting a whoosh of air escape his mouth. It had just been a dream!

He'd dreamt that he'd been naked at school, yet *again*. And for some very strange reason, no one had seemed to notice. He'd been terrified that at any moment someone would point out his nakedness and everyone would turn to look at him. Just as he was doing his best to hide under an impossibly narrow bench he'd woken up. He chortled to himself.

In general Kato liked dreams. The rules of the real world didn't apply in dreams, so he flew, rode on the backs of raging tigers, chased deer on foot and sometimes he even spoke, weirdly enough in Apu's voice. His favourite dreams, however, were those where he could tell that it was a dream while he was still in it. Then he knew anything was possible!

Not all of his dreams were about riding tigers and flying with the swallows though. There were occasionally skin-scorching, embarrassing dreams like the one he'd just awoken from.

There were also *other* dreams. He swallowed shakily as he remembered them. He'd dreamt them only a handful of times, each time when he was at a low point. They weren't *exactly* the same but they always happened in the same grey, damp, heavy, dead place. And he was always running from something, something unseen but terrible. In every one of them he was alone, and as much as he screamed the dead wind carried no sound. He never woke from these dreams and when the terror finally caught up to him, his last thoughts would always be a storm of terror and helplessness. He'd then pass out, and when he woke he'd always find himself lying on the floor.

Kato's breathing became laboured now and he shook his head to clear it of the acrid smoke that the dreams recalled. After a while his breathing returned to normal.

His attention returned to his mother's singing from the kitchen. The sound of a wooden ladle clunking against a heavy earthen pot became an apt accompaniment to her exquisite voice.

Khakhuli nanga je Shikhuli
Shikhuli nanga je Hevuli
Hevuli no azu pe-wu-ve
Shikhuli no alu chi wu-ve
Khakhuli akilo thi-wu-ve

He recognized the ditty; it was about an old woman, her daughter and granddaughter. The granddaughter was away fetching water and the daughter was toiling in the field while the old woman, left alone at home, goes away to the land of the dead.

Oishe! Oishe! Khakhuli na oishe! 'So sad! So sad! How very sad for Khakhuli.'

He went out and urinated on his mother's brinjal plants, making sure to be equally generous to each one of them. His mother would have stretched his ears out if she caught him, but as any naughty boy would vouch, the risk made it worth doing. After the wicked act was done, he smiled in satisfaction and sat on the wooden bench that his father had fixed towards the western side of their house, the side that faced the great mountain Thahakhu and its snow-capped peak. His parents would sit there in the evenings sometimes, talking in low murmurs, bathed in grey except for their hair that reflected the deep oranges of sunset.

Today the clouds were out in force and the cold wind against his skin told him that it would most probably rain. He thought that the procession of clouds looked like little piglets and fat sows rooting about in the mud.

He heard his mother calling for him and a moment later she came outside.

'Ilomi, my love, I've warmed water for you. Come, drink it and go down to the spring.'

He stayed there for a little longer, watching the clouds on their aimless meanderings, and went inside to fetch the long bamboo water containers, gleefully anticipating a day off from school.

'Pffff.' Kato's head and shoulder drooped in defeat, an abject figure with his satchel as he stood in the middle of the road. He'd just not been in the mood for school today, a perfect day for roasting sweet potatoes by the fireside! *What a waste*, he thought as he looked up dejectedly at the fast-retreating clouds. Lifting a leg, he flicked the stubborn mud lodged between his toes with a stick. The rain had been brief but long enough to make this slippery mess that made walking uphill a task. Usually, he walked around the village so he wouldn't have to meet people on the way, but today after the rain the soft earth on the sloping hillside presented too much of a challenge. He could see several other kids ahead of him, no doubt headed for the school too.

'It's a great shame!' the woman remarked. Kato lowered his eyes to the ground. The familiar voice carried all the spite its owner harboured inside her.

'Hmmm...' her husband agreed in a deep rumble.

'The way Nisheli tries to make that boy of hers act like a normal child. Anyone can see that he's not all there.'

'Aish! That's true, wife.'

Kato kept walking past the large thatch house outside which the man and his wife were standing.

Buoyed on by her husband's tacit approval she added, 'It would serve them both better to just accept reality and stop all this pretending.' Her voice increased in volume.

'Aish! Sending him to the school is just plain foolishness!' she continued after a pause. 'It's not like he'll be able to use anything he learned there when all he does is grunt like some beast. Spoils it for the other children and a terrible embarrassment to us! But that woman!'

'Aizaei! Aizei! Oh mother!' both of them concluded sadly looking right at him as he walked past.

Kato felt their eyes on his back, their 'tsk, tsk...' following him until he was out of earshot. As soon as he was out of their sight, he let out the hot breath of air he'd been holding in the whole time, the back of his ears tingling as though his mother had just pulled at them. His hands trembled like leaves as he replayed the conversation again, unable to decide which hurt more—that they'd blamed his mother for the way he was or that the man was his maternal uncle, his mother's only sibling, her older stepbrother who'd never had any fondness for either him or her.

A year ago, he would have refused to go on to school. A year ago, he *had* refused to go back. That first day the other children and the teacher himself had stared and stared at him, unable to make sense of his presence. He'd made it through that day, not lifting his head once, but simply refused to go back the next day. No threat or enticement would work. His mother had told him a story then.

Once there was a man who was the smallest man that ever did live. He was born when his mother drew her last breath, so he came out tiny and lacking life. People came to his home, and disregarding the sorrow of his father, they crowded in to look at the baby who was no bigger than a little squirrel.

So they say.

The tiny baby then became the smallest boy who stood no higher than your knees. The small boy then grew into the smallest man who ever lived—no taller than a three-year-old boy.

So they say.

Years later, the father of the little man also passed away, and he lived alone with his one-eared dog. He had no wife, for no woman would agree to marry such a small man.

One year the village chief announced the annual contest of the jhum field clearings. The prize would be an avi, a kind of gaur much coveted in the community. When the call was made for participants to present themselves, the little man walked to the front along with several other men, each tall, strong and fierce. Everyone was stupefied; it usually took a strong man at least three days to clear the fields alone and he was as small as a child.

But he stood his ground and neither the village chief nor his neighbours could talk him out of it. Everyone blushed in shame at his foolishness.

The day of the contest arrived. The contestants stood in front of their allotted spot and the buffalo horn was blown.

The contest began.

The other men, tall, fast and strong, started their work like raging bulls, clearing big swathes with one swing of their giant daos. The little man too began his work, but he was slow because his small hands could only hold a tiny dao. The area he cleared looked cleaner than those of the others for he was meticulous but by midday the others were way ahead of him.

When dusk came the others stopped working and went home, passing him on their way back, asking him to stop for it was late. But he continued wordlessly. Finally, under the moonlight, when his strength had completely ebbed, he looked up to find that he was still only a third of the way to the others. With a heavy heart he went home.

When he came back at dawn the next day, he was amazed to see that his patch was cleared to where the others had left the previous day! The other men were also amazed and looked at him strangely.

Things went the same way as the day before and the little man was left even further behind for the others worked with renewed vigour. Again, the other men left at dusk, and he stayed behind to keep working. But this time, under the moonlight, he only pretended to leave and hid behind a tree instead.

Shortly, a giant of a man came out of the trees and began to work on his patch with a curved hardwood that cut better than any dao. Before dawn, his patch was completely cleared.

They say a timi-ala had been watching him work from the dense jungle the previous day. So awed was he by the little man's determination and bravery that he decided to help him.

When the villagers came at dawn, they found the little man's portion completed, but he himself was nowhere to be found. They never saw him or his one-eared dog again.

So they say.

Kato was entranced by the story, the bad day at school completely forgotten.

'Oh! Did I mention that his name was Kato too?' his mother added, smiling to herself as she watched her son's awe-struck face. A bird could have nested in Kato's mouth, which was hanging wide open in shock and disbelief

He had gone back to school the next day.

<hr/>

Kato sat outside on his parents' bench watching the moonlit forest canopy stretching to the next mountain ranges and beyond. It was late and his parents were long asleep. Try as he might he could not quite forget the conversation between his uncle and aunt from that morning. His mind reached into the past.

'He can't speak?' the little girl had asked, peering at him from behind her mother's hekimini. 'Hush!' her mortified mother had exclaimed, pulling her ear. The girl began to cry and ran away. 'Stupid boy!' she'd stopped and shouted once far enough. Her mother stared at them in horrified silence.

'She's the stupid one,' she had apologized profusely to Kato's mother who wordlessly dragged him behind her faster than his little feet could keep up.

The distant memory was from when he'd been a three-year-old boy, still mumbling, unable to form a single coherent word. He clearly remembered the sight of his mother's tears streaming down her face as she carried him back home. He'd learned then that his muteness was something to be ashamed of, something he was *guilty* of. He began to feel the smallness taking root in him again.

Kato thought of the wee man and the smallness began to slowly retreat. *How I wish a timi-ala would come find me too,* he thought, questing out over the moonlit mountains with his eyes once again. Stories had always been his retreat, his solace, and tonight he wished they'd come true for him. An owl hooted from the forest below.

In the forests were trees so huge that it would take six men to encircle them; animals that made strange chilling sounds at night, their inhuman shrieks stealing into the uneasy dreams of people, making them murmur in their sleep; and brightly coloured flowers more lethal than vipers, which bloomed in deep ravines where no man had ever descended. In them were a thousand stories lying like seeds in the verdant ground, waiting to be carried away by someone who'd only dare to come find them.

After a while he went inside and soon sleep was upon him.

A knock came on Kato's door deep into the night when everyone in the village was asleep. It was soft but insistent.

The unfinished song that had hung above the lake a few days ago had come for him. It had truly begun.

3

The Beginning

The knocking began again, more insistent this time. *Thump thump thump!* The very last vestiges of Kato's sleep fled like tattered ghosts in a violent storm.

He burrowed deeper into his bed. There was no reason why a knock should scare him so. By any standards he was a brave boy. Many nights he'd stayed alone outside, looking at the forest below. Yet for some reason the knocks outside sent a chill through his body. *THUMP THUMP THUMP!* There it was again, loud enough to wake the dead this time! *It can't be someone from the village; a villager would have spoken up by now*, the calm part of his mind surmised. There was a dull solid depth that hinted at the great strength behind the quaint knocking. *Who or what else then ...* He shut his eyes tight and hoped for the knocking to stop, for whatever assignation waited outside to go away. But there it was again! *THUMP THUMP THUMP!* Maddeningly enough, his parents seemed to notice nothing and snored peacefully in their room.

His mind, lair of a terror-stricken imagination, began inventing the most frightening creatures—tall and gangly, dark and shadowy, limp and saggy, fanged maws and scaled tails, fiery eyes and putrid breath—of all sorts from the land of nightmares. He wanted to go to his parents' room but the thought of dropping his feet to the floor, exposing them to whatever might lurk under the bed, added one more nightmarish scenario to his over-burdened mind. *All the devils have come for me!*

He could hear his teeth chatter as he huddled inside his blanket. The terror reached into his guts and wrung them like his mother's laundry. His mind began frothing with numbing hysteria. But somehow, like fat in boiling water, like a stolen rooster poking its head through the thatch, the incurable curiosity within him began to nudge the insides of his brain. Hesitantly at first, it soon began to fight the terror so determinedly that the tension almost made him faint. *Go and look!* it screamed. He poked his head out of the blanket and listened intently, eyes darting one way then another.

Cagily, he tiptoed to the door and placed his shaking hands against the worn thatch. He put one ear against the door and listened, afraid to even breathe. *Hrmmm, hrmmmm, hrmmm…* whatever was outside sounded like an impossibly huge, obese housecat; the sound made his nose tingle with terror-laced excitement. When the knocking came again, he took a long, deep breath and shakily undid the twine latch. Bracing himself for the worst, he pushed the door open, not knowing that his world would forever be changed.

Something from his dreams sat outside his door. Kato swiftly clenched his eyelids shut and considered his situation. There was no going back. He couldn't simply shut the door and go back to his bed like nothing had ever happened. Whether he was to live or die he was *in* it. He opened his eyes.

It was still there.

Framed in the doorway sat a hunched figure that blotted out the stars behind. Strangely enough, he felt the beginnings of an irrepressible bout of incredulous laughter. It just seemed to be the most appropriate response to something so outrageous. Finally, the only thing he could manage was a weak *ummmpphhh*.

Blinking repeatedly, he looked up and down at the shadowy figure. From what he could see, it was humanlike, but so big that despite squatting half its head was hidden above the doorframe. This was no human.

'*Hrmmm, hrrrmm, hrrrmm,*' the shadowy mouth moved. It sounded like his father's snores, only much, much deeper, so much deeper in fact that it made the wood of the door tremble. He must have looked like a complete idiot, mouth gaping open, for even in the shadows he saw the mouth curve up in a smile.

'Come,' it said in a deep rumble that sounded like huge boulders rolling down a distant mountainside. Even the village chief's scary voice seemed like a child's in comparison. With no further instructions it stood up, leaving only its legs framed in the door, and turned to walk away.

Kato's heart pounded in his ears as he watched the giant amble towards the dip in the path further up. In the bright moonlight the scene looked like something from a lucid dream. So many times, he'd wished that the fantastic would come looking for him, and tonight it *had*! But now that it was here, he felt the queasiness of wading into the unknown, of being mere inches away from a sea of silent potentialities. He shivered. He'd just have to take *one* step back and shut the door, and the giant would leave him alone.

His heart now thundered like a furious herd of bulls. There, where the path curved away, might be the fearsome unknown but in the comfort of the house that called to him comfortingly was the same old life. In there waited the same boy who hid from people and grunted like the beasts.

A sob escaped his mouth, and he felt his heart squeeze painfully in his chest. Shutting the door firmly behind him, he raced towards the curve in the road.

———

The timi-ala—for he couldn't have been anything else—was so tall that even though he strolled leisurely Kato had to practically run to catch up. Peering down, it chuckled, noticing his problem and, reaching down with a gigantic vice-like hand, lifted him onto its shoulders as if he weighed nothing.

Perched there on the impossibly broad shoulder, Kato's teeth chattered like an old man's. He was so high! 'I won't mind if you hold onto my hair,' the giant rumbled. Kato obediently did so, grabbing onto the shaggy mane desperately. It suddenly occurred to him that the timi-ala spoke his language.

He felt a deep vibration and realized that his ride was humming. The potent scent of deeply worked earth and wet moss coming from the giant reminded him of his parents' field after a heavy rain. It was a smell that awakened dormant memories within him, memories that seemed to have no age. Perhaps a spell was being worked on him, but who could really tell. All he knew, all he cared about, was that he was being carried on the shoulder of a giant from the tales. His grin grew wider.

Before long they were passing between the carved village gates. Beyond it were the fields, and even beyond them, the great forests. Every step took him farther and farther away from the life he knew. Turning his head back he watched the familiar slopes of his village fall away. He hadn't considered the possibility that he might be taken away for good and the thought of it now sent a stab of fear through his heart. He calmed his mind recalling that nothing in the folk tales spoke of the timi-ala as abductors of people. That was the muza muza. Despite being the devourer of stories, it took all the faith he had in them to keep from panicking.

'Speak, little man,' the timi-ala said, interrupting his feverish train of thought.

'*He does not know I'm a mute,*' Kato thought, tripping inwardly in shame.

'Speak,' it said again.

Kato pointed to his lips and stuck out his tongue. He grunted, hoping to communicate his disability, but not with much hope because this was not his mother who understood his grunts and garbling. 'Speak,' the giant commanded, more firmly this time.

'I'm a mute. I canno…'

In complete disbelief, Kato lifted a hand to his mouth. From behind splayed fingers, afraid that it had been only his imagination he whispered, 'How is this possible?' He'd spoken in Apu's voice! To rule out the possibility that he was dreaming he pinched himself hard. It hurt enough for him to let out an agonized yowl.

The timi-ala laughed but said nothing.

The forest loomed in front of them, and the giant jogged the last few yards. The trees became a blur. Kato glanced back and once again he felt renewed fear sneaking in but it was far too late to do anything. Over steep inclines and into ravines they went. Around ridges, down chasms, up the sides of mountains—the timi-ala kept going on and on. Soon, they were in the thickest part of the forest; Kato could tell because the trees here grew taller than any tree he had ever seen on hunts with his father. The forest *sounded* different. It amplified even the smallest droplet of water and seemed expansive enough to swallow whole worlds. They passed a pangolin with her two pups, a herd of serow, a stray mithun, likely a naughty juvenile, and further on, its herd. The most numerous, however, were the foxes and jackals who followed a scent trail that they alone smelled. None of the animals seemed to pay them any mind, besides a curious lifting of a head here and there.

The giant finally slowed on reaching a grassy clearing and Kato was carefully lowered to the ground. He scanned his surroundings, half expecting something, or someone. There was no one else, just a huge boulder that seemed to somehow draw moonlight to it like sand does water.

'Ask your questions, little one,' the giant said. Kato slowly lowered himself to the grassy ground, his eyes still scanning his surroundings.

'Are you a timi-ala?' he asked.

The giant sat on the oblong boulder. 'What do you think?' it asked.

'How am I able to speak? Do you eat people?'

The giant put his hands on his belly and laughed, this time not soft and gentle but full and hearty. A wave of rustling and screeching ensued from the foliage around them.

Kato looked at his abductor closely this time. The giant couldn't seem to get over his mirth.

It was very tall, much taller than what Apu had claimed—now he knew for sure that his friend had made the story up. It would have taken four Katos to reach his ears and Kato was uncommonly tall for a thirteen-year-old boy. Even sitting, it dwarfed him by a great deal. It looked like a man but everything on it was just simply much too big. A tall man, like his father, was usually gangly and a little bowed, but this giant had limbs that were just as thick as they were long, and nothing about it was bowed or gangly. It was naked, its skin thick and hairy. The hair grew much longer and thicker below the hips, hiding its nakedness in a way. Its head was also much bigger than a human's, yet it looked a little undersized for its body.

Its face was thickly fleshed and had deep lines running across it with eyes that glittered behind thickset brows. Its nose was flat and generous. It looked like a face that liked to laugh and laughed often.

The giant was still laughing but the laughter had now ebbed into a low rumble. 'Little man, human meat is bland and stringy, and I wouldn't eat you unless I got very, very hungry,' it said with scarcely held in mirth. Kato gaped in horror and stood up in a hurry.

'No, we don't eat men,' the giant finally said in between guffawing. Kato exhaled with visible relief. 'As to how you can speak, it is not that you can really speak. I've merely allowed you to borrow some of my speech. When you go back to your own you will still be unable to talk.'

Kato felt disappointment bloom inside his chest like a leaking wound. He paced around glumly for a while, his relief from moments ago replaced by a new heavy feeling. *It was too good to be true anyway.* It did occur to him that it would be very strange to have two people speaking with the same voice in the village. 'Why am I speaking in Apu's voice?' he asked curiously.

'Perhaps you do not have your own voice yet,' the timi-ala replied.

'What a silly thing to say,' Kato thought. *How could a mute have a voice?* He decided not to press further, afraid that the giant may take away the voice if he made too much of it.

'What's your name?' he asked.

'*Your* name is Kato,' it stated instead.

'How did you know that?' Kato asked in genuine bafflement.

'I have big ears as you can see.' The giant laughed, making its huge ears twitch. 'I know a great deal from using these ears of mine.'

Kato stopped to stare at the huge ears, which were as big as taro leaves. 'What is your name?' he asked again. 'Do you have one?'

'Ah! My name,' the giant exclaimed as if he'd been asked for the first time. 'Yes… my name…' he drawled slowly like someone who was trying to bring up a long-forgotten memory. 'My name is Kene because I was made after Lakhe.'

'Kene, Kene,' Kato repeated to himself, liking the way it sounded.

Suddenly an epiphany dawned on him and he bounded up. '*Kini! Kini! Kini!* he shouted. 'That's two! Your name is two!' He sang and hooted as if he'd puzzled out the greatest riddle on earth. 'Kini, Kene, Kini, Kene…'

After a great deal of dancing and chanting he lay down on the grass exhausted. Kene sat on his boulder chuckling at Kato's antics.

'Why did you come to me?' Kato asked, 'I've always been told that timi-ala stayed away from people.'

'I need a storyteller,' Kene stated matter-of-factly.

Kato stared at him. *Is he mad?*

'Wwwhy?' he stuttered. 'You know that I'm a mute. I cannot tell any stories…'

'Trust me,' Kene said. 'There is no one better than you.'

Kato scanned the giant's face carefully, looking for any hint of mockery or deception. Being someone who couldn't speak, he'd developed a keen ability to read people's faces, to uncover what lay inside their hearts. But there was no mockery there. No hidden malice. He was stunned. Kene truly believed what he said. *Must be a fool.*

'But how am I to tell stories without a voice?' he asked.

'Ah!' Kene exclaimed. 'That is where you are wrong!' He stood up and walked over to where Kato was. Lowering himself on one knee he peered down at Kato's face. He stroked his head with a huge but gentle palm. 'A story is not simply in the telling of it.

'We'll make a deal, you and I,' he said pleasantly, sitting down now. 'I know how much you love stories.' Kato looked at him silently. 'I'll tell you the most amazing stories you've ever heard, take you on fantastic adventures.' Kato smiled, beginning to like where this was going. 'In return, I want you

to remember every one of my stories. Whether you are to be a storyteller or not we shall see when we get to it.'

'Is that all?' Kato asked. It seemed simple enough and he didn't sense any hidden entrapment. He knew enough about entrapments by fairies and otherworldly folk from the folklores to be careful.

'Yes,' Kene said smiling. 'But you MUST remember every one of them.'

Kato thought for a long time. It seemed like such an unequal exchange. Tonight had already proven to be the most exciting night of his life, and Kene was offering him so much more yet to come! And in exchange a mute boy simply had to remember stories? He was Kato, the devourer of stories. There was no doubt in his mind that he would remember every one of Kene's stories to a fault.

'Why do you need a storyteller?'

'Finally, you ask the important question!' Kene cried, standing up quickly. Kato's breath escaped with a *whoosh* as he was hauled up most unceremoniously onto the giant's back. 'For the answer to that question we must go higher,' Kene said busily strapping Kato to his expansive back with dry vine. It was snug but not tight enough to be uncomfortable.

Kato was still getting over his confusion when the giant began walking swiftly towards something that looked like a mountain. As they got closer, he realized with shock that it was no mountain but a gigantic tree! When they stood within touching distance it seemed even more unbelievable than Kene himself. Kato had seen other great trees before; even his village had a few. But this? He looked up at its height and nearly fainted as his eyes struggled to see to the top.

'This is Lakhe, my sister tree,' Kene said softly, reaching out and stroking the weathered bark. 'When I first came to be she was already a strong, tall tree.' Kene slowly pressed his cheeks against the bark and *hrrmmmed* tenderly.

'It *is* tall,' Kato said, feeling awkward, not knowing what else to say. The giant spoke of the tree as though it was a person and he felt self-conscious witnessing the tenderness between them. Kene leaned back and laughed his great laugh once more. 'That she is!'

All the shock that Kato had experienced tonight, or every other night in his life, couldn't have prepared him for what happened next. His eyes went wide when Kene's arms reached up and gripped the ridges that ran through the giant tree's bark. He'd done the same thing countless times with Apu and knew what was coming next.

'Hold still, little friend. I'm going to carry you to the clouds!' Kene shouted happily as he began climbing with a mighty heave.

Kene's arms swept up relentlessly over and over like a mighty swimmer, effortlessly projecting them upwards at a frightening pace. Kato shut his eyes tightly, prepared for a fumble, a slip, at any moment and then the inevitable fall to their gruesome deaths on the forest floor beneath. He began to regret ever following the giant to this place. When he finally mustered the courage to open his eyes the forest floor was a distant carpet visible only in the gaps between the branches. The cold wind and the terror made his eyes water, but he fought the urge to blink. The view was majestic. They were well above the forest, and he looked down at the earth as only the eagles do.

The great tree poked out like a rebellious child from the expansive canopy below. It was almost as if they'd crossed over to another world—the world of the angels, the kungumis. Up here the wind was strong and fast, making terrifying noises as it rushed past. They'd been climbing for a while but there was no sign of the giant tiring. There was no laboured breathing, no slowing of the powerful arms, only a joyful abandon that came out in little *whoop*s and *hooo*s. Before long they reached the top and

Kene set him down on the most unexpected thing—a very normal-looking platform built with logs and tied together with huge vines.

Kato had now moved beyond terror into a dreamlike state of wonder, and he wandered about the surprisingly steady platform. They were so high! Kene plucked a broad leaf off a branch. Rolling it into a funnel he scooped some liquid from a nook in a branch that Kato hadn't seen earlier in his fright.

'Drink this,' Kene said, handing it to him.

Kato hesitated for a heartbeat, not knowing what it was but he took it and drank deeply. It was water, but fresher and lighter than any water he'd ever drunk before.

'This is amazing! Is this some special kind of water?'

'You could say so,' Kene grinned. 'Lakhe is so tall that the clouds simply pass through her canopy. This is water that the clouds leave behind as gifts when they pass through.'

Kene strode forward towards the edge. 'Come, Kato,' he called. 'I will not let you fall.' Kato gingerly went and stood beside him.

'Look!' Kene said, holding out both arms as if in blessing.

Kato's eyes followed Kene's hands and what he saw cut short any questions he had.

Below them trees stretched into all directions, running unbroken for several leagues, interrupted only in the far-east by white-capped mountains. The clouds seemed low enough to touch. An owl hooted somewhere far below, and at once the unreality of it all hit Kato. Just this morning he'd been sitting in a classroom full of reluctant students trying to make sense of the squiggly patterns the teacher drew on the board, and now here he was with something out of his mother's stories perched on a tree that was as high as some mountains.

'Everything you see, even this great tree Lakhe, all of it, will change soon.'

Kato swung his head in Kene's direction. 'What do you mean!' he said incredulously.

'Come and sit beside me,' Kene said, gesturing to a nook in the trunk. 'I will answer your question now.'

'Have you heard of the long sleep?' Kene asked when Kato had settled himself in the nook.

'Can't say I have,' Kato replied.

Kene nodded. 'Of course, they wouldn't know... they're so young...' he spoke, looking away from him. Kato realized that the sentence was directed at the tree. He could almost swear the leaves rustled back in answer.

'It has been foretold,' he said, turning his attention to Kato again. 'It has been foretold that there will come a time when we must leave for a *long sleep*. Through many, many lifetimes of your people, we the *old ones* have known that the day would come.' He paused. 'And now, without a doubt, it is almost here.'

'How do you mean?' Kato asked.

'Very soon we, the old ones, will leave these lands and go away to the place that Alhou has prepared for us.'

'For the *long sleep*?' Kato asked.

'Indeed.'

'But what is this long sleep?'

'We do not fully know.' Kene took a deep breath and slowly exhaled through puckered lips. 'It isn't death as your people know it, that much I can tell, for we are to return someday. But whatever the case, we must go away for a long time.'

Kato fell silent. He found the thought of a land without Kene and the old ones exceedingly sad. 'Must you really go?' he asked finally.

'That much is for certain,' Kene replied. 'It is Alhou who has decreed it to be so, and we must obey. Disobedience has great costs,

'*That* is why I need a storyteller,' he added. 'We do not wish to be forgotten.'

'But of what use would your stories be when you are gone?'

Kene thought for a bit before answering, 'Kato, how would you feel if you found that everyone in your village had forgotten you while you were away with me?'

'Even my parents?'

'Yes, them too.'

When Kato *really* thought about it the idea became very disturbing. He imagined himself standing at his own door, his mother staring at him as if he were a stranger. 'I suppose I would feel like a ghost?' he said with an involuntary shudder.

Kene smiled at him approvingly. 'Memories are roots.'

'Roots?'

'Yes, roots. Everything that is living draws its life from the land. Without stories we have no memories and without memories our roots shrivel and die. It has been foretold that we, the old ones, must return from the long sleep one day, but without our memories, we will have nothing to return to.'

Kato nodded solemnly in understanding. *A people without stories disappear.* The Sumis too had their own saying. Another long silence followed. 'I still don't understand why you would choose a mute boy.' He looked down at the fresh dirt on his feet and wriggled his toes.

'Look here, little friend,' Kene commanded. Kato lifted his eyes and met the giant's steely ones. 'Once again I tell you, a story is much more than just the telling of it.' His eyes softened. 'When the time is right, I promise that you will understand,' he said gently.

Kato looked down at his feet once more and chewed the insides of his cheeks. He looked up after a while. 'Okay, I will do it.' His voice still lacked Kene's conviction but he met the giant's eyes without wavering.

'Say what?' Kene asked, leaning in closer and pretending to not hear. 'I will do it!'

Kato nearly fell over when Kene thumped him on the back. To his great alarm the giant began to whoop and clap, making the platform shake.

'We have a deal!' Kene said when he was done celebrating. 'You will be my storyteller and I will tell you stories and show you things you've never even imagined. Things you've never, ever dreamt of!'

His excitement was so infectious that Kato felt his own indecision falling away. His life was going to change. There would be amazing stories and adventures, and however things might end, nothing would take away from the fact that tonight the stories had come looking for him. Him!

'Tell me a story,' he told Kene.

'Tonight, it is enough that we've made a deal. There will be many other nights.' Kene said, eyes twinkling merrily. 'Why don't you just enjoy this perch that none of your kind has ever witnessed before?'

Hiding the speck of disappointment within, Kato nodded and obediently went back to looking out at the serenity of a landscape laid out like one of his mother's shawls. Below where they sat were countless animals, some small and frantic, some tall and strong, some that were purely deadly claws and teeth clothed in flesh and skin, and some that were all sinew, muscle and legless terror slithering between rocks and up trees. A shiver ran through him.

Kene began to hum a tune. It was not like the songs Kato's mother sang, as beautiful as they were. There were no words, just humming. Yet somehow it was more fleshed out, more expansive, much more than a tune. It was happiness from remembered sunny days, joy from deep gratitude, and a keen mourning for the passage of time that reduces all things to memories. The stars in the night seemed to draw closer as if to listen in and the cold breeze congregated on that branch high up on Lakhe's towering height. Kato wished he'd remembered to bring a shawl with him.

He found himself dozing, leaning against Kene's massive, warm arms. The incredibility of the night had finally caught up to him, sapping all of his energy in a moment of comprehension. He woke up long enough to mutter, in a sleep-drenched voice, 'Please bring me here again.'

The next morning he'd remember waking up in spurts to find himself cradled in Kene's huge arms, breathing in deeply the giant trees, musky animal smells and wet earth, feeling the world race by in this new, wonderful life and hearing the thump-thump of gigantic feet as they ran, and ran and ran…

4

Afterglow

*T*hud! *Thud! Thud!*

'Uuughhhh…' Kato groaned, squinting his bleary eyes at the slivers of dawn flitting in through the thatch.

Thud! Thud! Thud! He groaned again and massaged his aching head until the *thud* became a steady beat. All of a sudden, his half-waking mind jerked to attention, and he sat up in a hurry. 'Ouch!' He winced in pain as his nails dug into the soft skin on his wrist. *Was Kene just a dream?* He had no recollection of how he got to his bed.

But it couldn't have been just a dream!

Half afraid to hope and half in breathless anticipation he opened his mouth, working his tongue gingerly inside his dry mouth. What came out was not a string of intelligible words but his usual grunts and warbles. He felt a stab of disappointment, and strangely enough, embarrassment. He instinctively looked around, making sure that he wasn't being watched by anyone. 'Only when you are with me,' he remembered Kene telling him last night.

Now that he thought about it, the storyteller part did seem too far-fetched. *A mute boy of all people?* He cringed at the thought of telling anyone that a giant wanted him to be a storyteller—even his own mother would think him mad.

But something felt different this time. He couldn't say for sure what it was but unlike even the most convincing dreams the afterglow didn't feel like an echo but something much more substantial, something much more real.

Yet, what proof did he have?

Nothing. Nothing at all.

'Ilomi, please go down to the spring and fetch water,' his mother's voice from the kitchen halted his thoughts.

Scrunching up his eyebrows he inhaled a great, big breath and left for the kitchen with the very annoying feeling of having lost something.

The water gurgled as it filled the bamboo flutes, going higher and higher in pitch the fuller they got. He'd waited until the other folks left after filling their own water flutes, always preferring to do this alone. Even though the days had gotten positively warmer, the rock spring and the wet stone underneath were ice cold to the touch. After he'd filled his flutes, he lowered his head under the cold water and felt the coldness of the spring water making its way through his hair and drip onto his face, pooling together on his nose, and spilling onto the flat rock on which he stood, where they splashed onto his feet like tiny icicles. Satisfied that his mind was as fresh as it would ever be, he once again thought about the memories that crashed into his consciousness over and over.

No! It wasn't a dream! he told himself with a growl. It couldn't have been. Thinking the matter settled, he hung the heavy bamboo flutes onto the glistening carrying rod, burnished to a shiny glimmer from all the handling. Happily he lifted the rod onto his shoulder and scampered uphill to his home, leaving wet footprints on the earth.

'Ishou, you know what my mother told me?' Apu asked, swinging his sling bag alarmingly fast. Kato raised his eyebrows and murmured absently. Apu looked even more excited than his usual self. 'She said that some boys take longer to hit their growth spurt! You know, maybe I've not hit mine yet, you know.'

Kato immediately became attentive. He looked at his friend sideways and his heart ached at the hopeful desperation he saw on his face. Others may hit their growth spurts late, but Apu's had been right on time and had left him shortchanged. Kato recalled that Apu had almost caught up to him a little when they were younger, but then it stopped and then there was no more growing to speak of. Wanting to encourage Apu, he chortled merrily and thumped his back. His friend grinned at him, seeming to trust him fully, as was his nature.

A part of him desperately wanted to tell Apu about his adventure last night, but for some reason he felt that this was a secret he had to keep to himself. Kene would probably prefer it that way, even though he couldn't be sure how he knew. *Exactly!*—a thought within him began—*how do I even know it was real?* Irritably, Kato swatted at an invisible fly, trying to bat aside the errant thought.

The longer he walked with Apu, the more the sureness he felt at the spring trickled away. This was real, this moment with Apu, but what proof did he have of the impossible things from last night? Those times he'd dreamt of riding on the backs of tigers, of running with deer and flying with the swallows, none of them had continued to feel real after he woke up. Yet, this time he believed that a timi-ala, a giant of the forest, had taken him away last night!

By the time he reached the school Kato began to feel a right fool. *Talk with Apu's voice! Ha! Ridiculous!* he thought sullenly. Mournfully he closed his eyes and sighed as he took his seat inside the buzzing classroom.

Aghoto, the only teacher at the school, was a young man who'd been taken in by the missionaries as an orphan. At Impur, the first mission centre of the Christians in the Naga Hills, he had studied up to the fifth standard, which was quite an achievement. A kind and passionate man, he treated his work like a sacred vow, every class a mission. However, this very earnestness tired the children who only cared about laughing and playing, and didn't give two hoots about whatever his mission was.

Today, the teacher laboured without any gratitude as he tried to teach his raucous students that pronouncing elephant as 'illiphantu' would certainly not do. The students were still too busy laughing at the description of a creature with a nose longer than its legs. Apu as usual was being a clown, using an arm to act as his nose while he stomped around. Kato thought it was hilarious.

Aghoto finally had to threaten the students with calling the chief. This subdued them considerably since the chief was a fearsome man who put dread in the hearts of the children.

'Kato,' the teacher called after things calmed down.

Kato shrank back, instinctively making himself smaller.

'Kato,' the teacher called once more, louder this time. Kato stood up, eyes facing downward.

'Come up and spell "elephant" on the blackboard.'

Kato stayed glued to his place.

'Hahaha, can't even spell his name I'm sure,' a voice mocked. It was Yemishe.

Kato seethed inside. As a matter of fact, he knew exactly how to spell the word. His memory was sharper than anyone's in the whole class, and though he sat at the back, he paid close attention to every lesson.

'Quiet!' the teacher ordered. He glared at the place where Yemishe and his troublemakers sat. 'Yemishe, come up and write it then if you're so clever.' A long silence followed that was punctuated with many tittering and sniggering. 'Thought so,' the teacher said, throwing daggers at the offending group with his eyes.

'Kato,' he spoke gently. 'I know you can do this. Come up.'

Kato didn't move. His head buzzed like it held a million bees.

'Come up,' the teacher coaxed.

'Idiot.' Barely louder than a whisper, Kato heard it come from the same spot.

'The pig's ass!' Apu hissed under his breath angrily.

Biting down hard Kato lifted his head. He'd not intended to go forward but the word inflamed him and before he knew it his feet had begun moving. The disappointment of finding that his fascinating adventure had been merely a dream became a fire that fuelled the anger within. He felt Apu's hand thump him on the back encouragingly.

The walk to the blackboard felt like it had taken the whole day.

'Here,' Aghoto said, handing him the chalk.

Inhaling shakily, Kato lifted the chalk. He noticed his hand trembling. All his focus and strength went into holding his hand steady, and he barely knew what he was writing. When it was done he dropped his hand quickly.

'Very good!'

Kato finally remembered to exhale and felt unending relief sweep over him. Handing back the chalk, he found the teacher smiling at him proudly.

After the painful walk back he lowered himself on the bench, only to be grabbed in a great hug by Apu.

'Who's the idiot now?' his friend gloated, making sure that the whole class heard him.

'Silence!' the teacher barked, this time with a satisfied smile instead of a glare.

Kato leaned back against the cold earth watching his left feet draw imaginary circles on the boulder. He was in his special place by the river, a small nook formed by a big boulder wedged into an abrupt bend along the riverbank. The space between the boulder and the bank was just enough for a boy his age to curl up, away from peering eyes. He'd hoped that the sound of the river would seep into his mind and drown out his worries about the too-real dream, but to his great irritation, they proved to be like a stubborn sinew stuck between two molars.

A sudden anger began building up inside him. If Kene was only a dream, why would his mind not stop drumming and simply forget about it like he did other dreams? The tension of it all came to a boil and, overcome by frustration, he went to the river and began to frantically push boulders into the rushing torrents. *'Take it back! Take it back!'* his mind screamed as the boulders sank into the river one by one.

After the fifth boulder he stopped keeping count. His shoulders and back ached from all the pushing but mercifully now the pounding of his heart was all he could hear.

As he lay gasping he caught sight of his old friend slinking around the other side of the river. Its jet-black hair glistened under the afternoon sun and the wetness of its nose was adorable. Of all the creatures he saw down by the river the small, muscle-bound otter was his favourite.

It was a terribly smart thing, the otter. Using its tiny paws, it would hold the fish it caught and eat them while lying on its back. Kato wished that the hunters in his village would never catch it. Now it stood on its hind legs between the roots of a tree, speckled by the shadows of the leaves before it disappeared into the foliage.

It reminded him of Ihe, his pet dog, who had died four years ago. A gift from his grandmother, he'd raised her from a puppy. She'd been black like the otter, with a little white patch on one eye. Ihe had followed him everywhere and for three years they'd been inseparable. One day, while foraging for wild berries in the valley, they'd come across a very angry viper. He still remembered the flash of action like a blur—the viper drawing back its head and Ihe leaping forward, placing herself between Kato and the snake's fangs. In a blink it was done and he watched helplessly as the snake slithered away into the dense foliage.

He had said no to getting another puppy ever since. What was the point anyway? He'd have to say another painful goodbye no matter how long it took.

He sat on the sandy bank for a while longer, mourning a memory that still felt all too real. *Two memories, actually.*

———

Even before he set foot inside, he could smell the scent of roasting corn coming from the kitchen. His mother was back from the field. His mouth watered at the thought of juicy corn browned into shining, pitted kernels of goodness and tastiness.

She saw him come in and smiled. It was a decent-sized Sumi kitchen—squarish and very unmistakably built around the generous round hearth at the centre. The thatched walls were blackened with soot, and utensils of all sorts were hung from beams and arrayed on shelves that decked the sides. Unhusked corn, long plaids of garlic, strings of chillies and other vegetables hung within easy reach, and above the fire a wooden frame hung from the ceiling—a very important component, one could even say *the* most important component, of a Sumi kitchen. This frame held a very loosely woven bamboo mat and was used to smoke meat, fish and axone.

For a Sumi to call axone a condiment or ingredient would be akin to calling water an ingredient in cooking. It was made by pounding boiled soyabean, wrapping the sticky result in taro leaves and slow-smoking it over a fire so that fermentation could happen while imbuing the unique smoky taste and smell. Very divisive in its appeal, to some it might appear and smell utterly revolting, but to a Sumi who knew the process from start to finish, it was the most wholesome, appetizing brown paste known to humanity. It would be no exaggeration to say that at all times any self-respecting Sumi kitchen would have axone, if nothing else.

'Apuza sends you her love,' she said.

Kato grunted in acknowledgment but all his attention was on what the fire contained. Five cobs of corn lay haphazardly, resting on the burning wood, and Kato watched as they slowly reddened under his mother's constant ministrations. His mouth watered.

'How was school?' she asked.

He stuck two fingers against his forehead. *Good.* They had their way of communicating. His mother smiled in approval. He smiled too, remembering his rare moment of triumph.

'You must be learning so much, no? I wish I could learn to read and write too but I'll have to wait for you to teach me.'

Kato giggled at the thought of him teaching his mother without words, but he knew she was just trying to make him feel better about school.

One cob of corn seemed to be done and Kato quickly pointed it out. His mother retrieved it from the fire with a tong and wrapped it in fresh cornhusk before handing it to him. He held the steaming goodness under his nose and took a long sniff, closing his eyes in pleasure as the scent filled his entire brain. Venturing his thumb and forefinger he pulled one kernel out of the cob and popped it in his mouth, only to spit it out as it scalded his tongue.

'Aish! Don't be so impatient. Couldn't you have waited for a while to let it cool?'

Chastised, he blew on it frantically, wishing for it to cool faster. She giggled like a little girl and pulled him close, smudging her cheeks up against his until he groaned and struggled to get away. Having extracted himself from her clutches he made a seat for himself on the other side of the hearth, away from her, and began chomping contentedly.

―――

Afterwards, with the corn all eaten and his clothes changed, he went outside and watched lightning streak down over a valley to the west. There it was raining so hard that even from up here it looked misty and diffused, yet here there was not even a single droplet to speak of.

After an hour or so the wind brought the rain clouds over his village and it began pouring down like heaven's own wrath, driving people inside their homes—and outside, streams and rivers of muddy water.

Down by the river Tapu, a sleek otter slid back into the hole it had made its home in no hurry, a half-eaten fish clenched between its teeth. Unlike the hairless creatures in the village, it wasn't afraid of rain.

5

Ipuza

GRANDMOTHER

Kato swung the stout stick like a weapon. If a tiger came out of the bush just then he'd get a good wallop on the head, he thought, feeling quite brave. His face scrunched into a fierce expression as he imagined his moment of triumph.

Today, he was on his way to his grandmother's. 'Don't ask so many questions, my love,' his mother had told him. 'Just go and see your grandmother.' He *knew* something was afoot, but he loved visiting his grandmother anyway. There would be yummy stuff to eat, and stories! Lots of stories!

'Take a look at your Apuza's firewood stock!' he heard her shout almost out of earshot as he sped up the mountain.

There were three paths that would take him to his grandma's. One was the village path, a network of serpentine paths that crisscrossed the village that everybody used. Another was the one that he and Apu took to school, but the quickest was the one that he was on today. If it had been anything else but a sunny afternoon, he wouldn't have taken this path. Even though he considered himself reasonably brave, the burial grounds were a peculiar sort of eerie, and while the path did not go directly across them, it was still close enough to discourage a boy from taking it under moonlight or even cloudy greyness. Even now under the bright sunlight with the chattering of birds he could feel the beginnings of something queasy deep within his belly.

Merely steps from the clearing towards which he hurried, a rustling in the bushes to his left made his blood freeze. While he was debating whether to run or prepare to fend off whatever horror lurked there, a very dishevelled figure of a woman stepped out just in front of him.

It was Ghonili, the village Tu-Umi. The *witch*.

Kato held the stick in front of him, his tongue suddenly heavy and bloated. The witch, however, seemed to have not even seen him as she brushed cobwebs and leaves from her hair. At this lack of anything resembling a threat he slowly lowered the stick, but his relief was a moment too soon for she suddenly stopped whatever she was doing and stared straight at him. The fear from moments ago swelled in his chest again.

The witch chortled in merriment at his pale face and moved closer until she was inches from him. She was so close that Kato was surprised when no offensive old, musty smell harassed his nose.

He saw that her clothes were just very discoloured and worn, perhaps even deliberately made to look older, but she was in fact cleaner than some villagers. It was simply the colour and age of her hekimini and the shade of grey of her hair that gave her the appearance of being dirty. Another thing that surprised him was that she was younger than she looked from afar. Probably not much older than his grandmother, despite the rumours of her being more than a hundred years old.

His eyes opened wide, and his nose flared when she lifted a hand and stroked his face. The stick in his hand felt like it weighed a ton, and though he wanted to hit her with it and run away his body seemed frozen to the ground.

'Little squirrel' she drawled. He stiffened up even more; only his mother and grandmother called him that.

'Did you know that a kingfisher stole your tongue when you were a baby?' she asked, laughing gleefully. Then, suddenly, she turned and hurried away towards the burial grounds, leaving him feeling both terrified and confused.

He ran so hard that by the time he reached his apuza's home he was gulping air like a floundered fish. In his mad haste to get away, he had tripped and fallen down a small gully, making him look just as dishevelled as Ghonili had been. There were also bruises on his face and elbows.

His grandmother came out of the hut where she'd lived for as long as he remembered. Her face broke out in a grin when she saw his state.

'Ghost chase you, little squirrel?' she asked, not realizing how close she'd come to the truth. 'What a state you're in, boy! Your mother would have a fit if she saw you now.' She chuckled as she examined his face and turned his body around to judge the seriousness of his wounds. Grandmothers always seemed to let you get away with much more than mothers, he thought happily.

'You'll live, it looks like. But come anyway and let me apply some pig fat and you'll feel better.'

True to her words, he did feel much better after her attentions. Sitting by her as she baked sweet potatoes in the hot ash of the kitchen fire, he thought of how lucky his mother was to have grown up in the home of this wonderful woman.

Mostly recovered now, he sat on a small asu-lakhu, a wooden bench just a little taller than one's ankle. His grandmother was at the loom where she wove something ebony-coloured. One elbow propped on a knee, he thought about the Tu-Umi while chomping on a sweet potato. *What a strange thing to say. Could a kingfisher really steal people's voices?* It didn't make any sense. *But Kene did let me speak by borrowing his voice.* Hurriedly he corrected himself—*that was just a dream.* After some more thought, he dismissed the whole thing as the ravings of a mad woman. His grandmother cleared her voice, and he looked toward the weaving loom. She unhooked the belt that went around her lower back and stood up.

'A story then?' she asked.

Kato answered with emphatic claps and whoops. His grandmother smiled wryly and brought a bamboo chair over to him. Tussling his hair fondly she began.

'My father, your great-grandfather was a mighty man, renowned hunter. This is about one of his hunts into the great forest beyond Thahakhu, the highest mountain in the region.'

Oooohhh! This already sounded like a great story! Kato crossed his arms and rubbed his sides in barely contained glee. Hunters always seemed to have the most amazing stories, and his maternal great-grandfather was a larger-than-life figure who still came up in village conversations, many years after his passing.

'Countless hunters have gone into the forests, and yet they remain as unknown as they ever were. The stories these hunters bring back are simply dots in the dirt, and when they've gone back to their warm, dry homes, the forests still hold their secrets tightly unto themselves.'

Kato was already under the sway of his Apuza's words. His mother had surely gotten her storytelling skills from her mother.

'This is one of the many stories your great-grandfather brought back with him, but this one is special.' That surely was a hook to a story if ever there was one! 'Do you know why?' Kato shook his head, mind buzzing with probable scenarios, each fantastic but none seeming to come close to justifying the suspense his grandmother had created. 'It was his last.'

Kato's eyes grew wide as he sunk deeper into the spell of the story that had not even begun.

'Some hunters go in pairs, some in threes, seldom more. Animals have noses sharper than us and their ears hear the folding of leaves, and many feet drive the prey away. It is however the rare hunter who goes alone into the great forests for they have a power that dwarves the souls of people and only the bravest can sustain their courage alone. My father, your great-grandfather, a *man* among men, always went alone on his hunts much to my mother's distress.

'He'd been on many hunts before and he'd always be back within two or three days but this time he was nowhere in sight even after four days. My mother became increasingly sick with worry and the village chief was on the verge of calling for a search, as futile as that would be knowing how deep into the great forest he would go, when on the fifth morning he stumbled into the village looking like a ghost.'

Kato pulled the small stool closer to his grandmother and rested his chin on her knee. He could feel the story building. A discerning patron, he felt the story's flow as keenly as if it were a living thing. Eyes wide with wonder he looked up at her.

'How he came to look like that the villagers could only guess, for he went straight home leaning on my mother, and after a long drink of water promptly fell asleep. He lay like that burning with fever for two nights and an entire day.

'Would you like to know what he said when he woke up?'

Kato nodded furiously, quite bewildered at what his grandmother found so amusing that she should laugh at him now.

'Oh, my little squirrel! How I love you!' she said as she reached out and stroked his cheeks, just like the witch had done earlier.

'He told a story that was fantastic and horrifying all at once.' She paused here, as storytellers often do. No longer able to contain the suspense he lifted his head and stared at her open-mouthed. 'He'd had no luck and by the second day he had strayed farther into the forest than he ever had before.'

Here the story became so powerful that Kato was transported to the little dim room of his great-grandparents from many years ago. He became one among the many awed faces that crowded the hut, and almost as if in a trance he saw his great-grandfather open his mouth and speak with the voice of his apuza.

I've come home empty-handed from other hunts before but this time…

On the second day I still had nothing to show for my efforts… I trailed further into the forest. Much further than I have before, perhaps much further than anyone in the village ever has.

I picked up the trail of a herd of wild boar and began to follow it…

I followed them to a watering hole. Ten adult boars and three piglets. I made camp high on a tree… was going to set a snare when they left to forage during the day.

It was the third day and I was very tired… more tired than I ever thought I'd be. I slept through the evening and the whole night. Sometime in the early hours of the morning I was woken by the sound of great splashing. It was light enough that I could see what was happening…'

His complexion paled, and he asked for water. After taking a long drink he continued, chest heaving as though he'd been underwater for a long time.

'A giant python... *Ayithu amiche-kupu-u!*' His face blanched in such terror that his wife, thinking he was going to faint, ran to his side. He mustered courage and licked his dry lips.

'It was so big that the water hole looked like a puddle from which it drank. Its body that never seemed to end coiled and uncoiled again, all muscles and sinew. Its terrible head was as big as our village gate and a black crest ran down the middle.'

The whole audience gaped in wonder for there were stories of such a serpent but today they were hearing a first-hand account.

'I've seen great pythons but this one dwarfed them all. After it had drunk its fill, the water hole was half dry. It lifted its head high in the air, as high as some trees... tasting the air with its purple tongue; my heart beat so loudly that I was afraid that it would learn of my presence. After what seemed like a very long time it slithered away into the forest.

'I was so terrified that I couldn't find the courage to climb down even though it had left a long time ago. My spirit couldn't overcome the sighting and I lay like one dead, until finally after a whole day I finally climbed down and made my way back here.'

'He never went on his hunts again.' The words ended the thrall of the story and Kato was brought back to his grandmother's kitchen. 'Lesser men would have given up their spirit, but my father was brave and so his spirit recovered to an extent, but going back into the forests was something even he could not manage anymore.

'Something he told me many moons later always stayed with me. *Such a serpent could swallow the moon.*'

Kato climbed down the small drop into a shoulder area of the mountain. He was within shouting distance of his grandmother's house. Unslinging his cane basket, he took the dao and a rope out and surveyed the cluster of trees. Carefully he tied one end of the rope to the dao and the other end around his waist. Picking a tree that had dead branches, he climbed swiftly and pulled the dao up, being careful not to get cut himself. Perched securely, he began to chop with strong, steady swings. *Thunk, thunk, thunk*... the sound echoed over the mountainside. After a while, another echoing *thunk* began further down, and it amused Kato to turn it into a game with him following immediately after the other one.

When his branch went crashing down to the ground, he sat on the branch he'd been perched on and leaned against the trunk. Questing his eyes over the mountainside he perked his ears up and tried to pinpoint where the sound was coming from. From the deep sounds of the *thunk*s he could tell that it was an adult, a strong adult. They stopped for a while, and he smiled knowing that the other person had also been playing his game and was waiting for him to continue. After a while it began again, and Kato felt a little sorry at having to disappoint his unknown partner. It occurred to him that if he'd been face to face with the other person, he'd never have started the game.

Kato felt a shiver climb his spine as he looked at the biggest tree there. Lakhe! The sounds from further down stopped and now there was only the sound of the wind, the creaking of bamboo and the occasional faint sounds of little children playing that was carried by the breeze. He closed his eyes and concentrated on the wind against his skin and the distant sounds of the children; he could imagine that he was up on Lakhe the great tree that night. *Just a dream,* he reminded himself again, but a queer feeling climbed down his spine and he felt a very sudden, urgent need to urinate. Quickly he climbed down and emptied his bladder.

The basket was quite heavy with chopped wood and he was huffing by the time he reached his apuza's hut. This was his fourth and final trip to the tree. *She'll be fine for a good while,* he thought happily as he added the wood from the basket to the woodpile under the small shed.

'Little squirrel,' he heard her call from inside. 'Come in and have chicken soup'. He looked up at the sky and shook his head in amazement; the sun was already dipping in the west. He hung the basket under the sheaves and went in after washing himself.

The queer feeling on the tree had awakened memories and he thoughtfully spooned the chunks of chicken into his mouth. 'Here,' his grandmother said, and he looked up immediately because the promise of something nice dripped from her voice. 'For being a very good boy,' she said with warmth as she produced something from behind her.

The shawl was the most beautiful thing Kato had ever seen, and it fit him perfectly—black as night with a single crimson line, the width of three fingers, running through it.

It wasn't one of the *known* shawls that the Sumi used. There were several, the kichimi qhumi, asu-kuda qhumi, avi-kiyi-phi. Each shawl signified something and could only be attained after meeting strict conditions. The kichimi qhumi could only be worn by men who'd crossed into adulthood, so also the avi-kiyi phi could only be worn by people who'd completed their feast of merit, the asu-kuda qhumi only permitted to those who'd performed acts of valour in battle, the cowries sewed onto the shawl representing the number of feats they'd performed. If anyone wore them without qualification they'd be excommunicated from the village and fined heavily. It was taboo, and they'd be inviting curses on themselves and their family. Similarly, the women also had their shawls and hekimini. Kato's was something completely new.

'Only you have this shawl,' his grandmother half whispered. 'None other.'

Kato swallowed hard, still marvelling at its beauty.

'You see this?' she asked, pointing at the bold line running across the ebony black of the shawl. He nodded, hastily wiping his hand on the floor. 'This is your will, your anguagha. It is the quality that makes your spirit strong or weak.' Kato stared at the line woven into the cloth, unrelenting and defiant. 'Now this here,' she waved her hand over the black parts, 'is your lot in life.' She cupped his hand and made him look at her, 'Good, bad, happy, sad… we very rarely get to choose,' He swallowed hard and reached out to trace the line with two fingers. 'You understand? It is your anguagha that will take you through it all. So, make it strong and bold like this line here.' She pulled him in close and hugged him, the shawl caught between them, both of their hands tightly clutching it.

'You take care of this now, you hear?' she instructed him later, to which he nodded his head vigorously.

When he got home it was close to dusk, and soon, more silent than a crafty hunter, night spread its long arms around the village.

6

Mozaqhi: Weeding Month

MAY

The clearing cycle for the rice fields was in full swing. Kato went to his parents right after school, glad to be out among the jhum fields. The stalks of rice were now ankle high, and the air was pregnant with their scent. He stood atop his parents' field, closed his eyes, drew in a deep breath through his nose and *aaahhhed* in pleasure.

For nearly four hours he worked beside his parents on the slopes of the jhum fields, using rake and hands to find malevolent weeds while they were still barely shoots themselves. Given even a little time they'd climb up the rice stalks and overrun them completely within days. His fingers were sore and his nails had dirt packed tightly underneath them.

In the end, despite their fatigue and aching backs, they went back home with the satisfaction of knowing that they'd held the threat of the suffocating weeds at bay, even if it was just for a few more days.

'Uuurrrggghhh!' Kato exclaimed in pain. A splinter had entered one of his fingers just beneath the nail, making it hard for him to even eat. His mother was feeling for the invisible assailant with her tongue. 'There you are!' she exclaimed when she felt the teeny prick on her tongue. Deftly she extracted it with her teeth and made him soak his finger in hot salt water afterwards. Still, it hurt like a bee sting.

After dinner his parents spent a long time talking about the news that was the talk of the whole village. Kato lay down on a rug in front of the fire, letting his imagination paint pictures for him in the fire as he listened to them talk.

'… not another story I hope,' his father said, leaning back on the lone wooden bench he was sharing with his wife. They sat close together even though it was big enough for three adults. 'I hope not,' his mother acquiesced. 'Salushe and his stories!' She threw back her head and laughed. Salushe was Apu's father, and everyone knew father and son shared the same love for tall tales. Kato smiled thinking of his friend.

'He seemed quite worked up,' Kato's father said.

After a long pause, his mother let out a whoosh of air. 'A leopard in the village though! How exciting!'

'Hush now!' his father scolded. 'You know as well as I do that a leopard would never venture into a human village unless it was desperate. Probably wounded… If it is true then our children and old folk wouldn't be safe.'

A little mollified, his mother replied, 'I suppose you're right... but still!' She looked like an excited child. His father harrumphed in mock disgust.

Kato fell asleep, lulled by the warmth from the fire and the faint sound of his parents' conversation.

'Wake up, son.'

Kato opened his bleary eyes, shaken awake by his father. He looked around to find his mother pouring ash on the glowing embers of a spent fire, a necessary precaution for those who live in thatch houses. Eyes half closed, he groped his way to his bed and promptly fell asleep.

—

In the dreamscape of Kato's mind, as he was trying to reach out and catch a dream that had left too soon, something entered his consciousness. It seemed vague but familiar, distant yet inexplicably insistent. The dream he'd been trying to apprehend faded away, and in a moment of startled recognition his eyes flew open.

'Wake up little man,' a spectacularly deep voice said from outside his door.

This time there was no hesitation; all he felt was exhilaration and such a strong sense of vindication that it brought tears to his eyes. 'It was not merely a dream!' Pausing only to grab the shawl his grandmother had woven for him, he unbolted the door and ran outside. Kene stood there, hands on his hips, smiling like a kind old uncle.

'Come,' was all he said. Kato braced himself for the lift as the giant effortlessly hauled him onto his shoulder.

'I thought you were a dream,' he said hesitantly as Kene started walking. It had been several days since the last time and while he was elated that the giant was here, they were practically still strangers. Apu's voice came as a shock to him again despite his joy. He grinned happily realizing that every other detail, like Lakhe and the platform on her heights, was true too. He couldn't wait to look down at the earth like the eagles once again!

'Hmmm...' a deep rumble reverberated from his ride. Kato stared at him with a puzzled look, unable to decide whether that was the answer, or he'd have to repeat what he said. 'I said I thought you were a dream,' he repeated. 'Hrmmm...' a deeper rumble came. Kato scrunched his eyebrows, a little irritated, but the sudden realization that Kene wasn't just another person but a giant hit him; there was no point taking offence at things like politeness or good manners.

'Where are we going tonight, Kene? To your sister tree?'

'No, not sister tree tonight. Tonight, we go to watch a certain someone.'

The mention of a 'someone' had Kato's curiosity out in an instant.

'Who? Is it a man? Is it another timi-ala?' he asked breathlessly.

'No, *she* is neither man nor one of my people. You will see...you will surely see.'

'Oh! Come now! It can't be such a secret if you're taking me to watch her!' Kato said petulantly. Despite their lack of familiarity he couldn't help feel that this abruptness was a side that he'd have to deal with frequently.

'Wait, impatient little man, wait. Such impatient folk you men are!' Kene exclaimed, sounding very much like his mother did when she was at the end of her patience. 'But I suppose since you live only so briefly that's understandable.'

Kato withdrew into sulking as their shapes merged into the inviting solidity of the blackness that was the forest. Despite his irritation, he couldn't stave off the excitement. *If only Apu were here to watch me!* He gleefully imagined how the fellow would gape and be awestruck.

'Whom are we going to watch, Kene?' he asked a good thirty minutes or so later.

'Soon, my little friend, soon.'

They passed a small herd of deer, and once a pair of wild mithun who paused briefly from drinking at a mountain spring to look before going back to drinking again.

'You called for me tonight. What if you woke my parents and the other villagers?' Kato asked, resigned to the fact that this giant would not be spilling details no matter how hard he prodded.

'They wouldn't because I did not mean for them to hear,' Kene replied, still talking in riddles. 'How do you think, that despite so many human hunters roaming my forest, I've managed to stay hidden for so long?'

'How? Tell me then,' Kato said, fed up of all the riddles.

Kene replied, 'Why, I know how to make myself heard, and also how to make myself unheard, and unseen.'

'You can become invisible then?' Kato gawked in disbelief.

'I don't know what you mean but if I chose to, I could be sitting on that log right in front of you and you wouldn't know I was there.'

'Show me then.'

'Why would I do that?' Kene asked, looking genuinely bewildered.

Kato harrumphed but kept his cool. Their first meeting hadn't been anything like this. Somehow it felt as though they were tripping over each other's feet this time around.

A while later, Kene began to climb a small mountain, but this time he picked his way up much more carefully. When they reached the top, he lowered Kato down gently. Leaning down close he whispered in Kato's ear, 'Be quiet now and follow me.'

Kato obeyed for once and threaded his way gingerly behind Kene, making sure he was as quiet as possible. They climbed a little ways downhill before Kene gestured for him to stop behind a line of firs, beyond which was a sheer drop. Kene sat down on the ground and Kato followed his lead, sitting close beside his giant friend.

'Now be quiet and look down there in the ravine.' Kato peered down, and in the bright moonlight he saw a pool of water at the bottom, and beyond it a clearing in the forest. But there was nothing else.

'Where is it?' Kato asked. His insides were in a churn with all the secrecy and suspense.

'She comes, she comes. Just be quiet and watch!' Kene snapped.

It's a person then, Kato thought, feeling a little chagrined.

A while passed before anything happened.

'Now she comes!' Kene exclaimed, as much as a person can exclaim while still whispering. The giant looked like a child who could barely contain his excitement.

Kato heard it before he saw anything—the sound of many hooves and with them a voice, 'Ahooooyyyyy! Ahooooyyy!'

A small figure stepped into the clearing. It looked like a child, not much taller than Kato, but it moved in a way that was more animal than human. It looked around, seemingly scouting the area. Apparently satisfied, it raised its hands to its mouth.

'Ahhooyyy!' it called. A moment later a huge herd of deer, boar and other smaller animals moved into the clearing and began to drink from the pool.

The small figure leapt on a rock and began to swing something that looked like a long, thin branch in the air. It made a sound that went *whhhiiiittttt*, like the sound a whip makes.

'*Ahai! Ahai! Ahai! Ahai!*' it shouted in time with the wide swings.

Kato was speechless with wonder as he watched what was happening below. What was a child doing in the deepest part of the forest? Why were the animals following it?

'Shi-kheu,' Kene said reverently.

Kato's eyes went wide. The old tales spoke about a guardian of the wild whom the animals followed from place to place. There wasn't a single Sumi who didn't believe that they were real, from the oldest to the littlest one. However, the old days were receding quickly— chased away by the coming of the white man, by half pants and squiggly letters on blackboards.

He had thought at first that it was a human child but the thought seemed most absurd now—no human child was as hairy as the shi-kheu, and a human child definitely did not have just three fingers! Even from up here it was clear that it had two forefingers that were a little larger and longer than a human's, and one big thumb that was almost as long as the fingers. The hair on its body seemed especially longer around the back of its arms, legs and back. The head was aquiline like a badger's, but it still looked human enough for Kato to have mistaken it for a child before. It also paused frequently to raise its nose and sniff at the wind, like wild animals do.

Kato watched the shi-kheu in spellbound silence. It was beautiful to watch, its movements not at all human-like, lacking any of the awkwardness of a bi-pedal creature. While he marvelled at this child-like creature that prowled below them like a feline king, a realization dawned on him that was immediately followed by a certain kind of pathos. Despite all its beauty, it was alone— like Kene.

A curious fawn strayed away from the herd towards the west, but a sharp crack of the branch with a '*hei, hei, hei!*' brought it scuttling back.

The shi-kheu looked in their direction, swung its whip three times— *Whit! Whit! Whit!*—followed by a long ululating cry. Its amber eyes seemed to look straight at Kato, and he drew back involuntarily, fear replacing the pathos from moments ago.

'Does it know we are here?' he whispered frantically.

'Of course. She smelled us when we were still mountains away.'

'Then why all the careful walking and silence?' Kato asked sourly.

Kene peered down at Kato, looking disappointed. 'Because we must respect her, little man.'

Kato felt his face flush in embarrassment and shut his mouth.

The shi-kheu leaped down from the rock and, with one final look in their direction, led its animals away into the forest from where they had come.

'*Ahooooooyyy! Ahooooooyyy!*' The cry came to them as they melted back into the trees. After a while its cry began to sound like echoes, and soon echoes of echoes, and finally only the sound of leaves rustling in the wind.

'Is it the owner of the animals?' Kato asked, still battling disbelief.

'No, no not the owner. Their caretaker, you could say,' Kene replied.

'All the animals in the forest?'

'The ones with fangs and claws walk their own trail, but even they will listen to her.'

'But that was just one herd, what about the rest of the animals in the forest? Surely, there are countless more!'

Kene looked pleased. 'You have the right questions, my friend. You see, the animals know the shi-kheu and obey her. All she does is move on to another place, and where she goes the animals there come to her.'

'Whoa!' Kato exclaimed. 'How does she keep track of them all?'

'Why, she's their caretaker, so of course she knows each one of them.'

Kato narrowed his eyes and thought about it. It didn't make sense yet after what he'd just witnessed; Kene's answer somehow worked. With a click of his tongue, he decided the matter settled and turned his attention to the giant.

'Kene, how many shi-kheu are there?' He looked down at the deserted watering hole that had been teeming with animals and a kingly being just mere moments ago.

'Oh, not many, but enough,' Kene replied.

'What sort of an answer is that?' Kato guffawed with raised arms. After the hilarity subsided, he tilted his head and gave Kene a wry smile. 'You do not know how to talk. Do you really not talk to anyone else beside me?'

'I *talk* to many others beside you, but in the way you and I talk? There's just you,' Kene replied seriously. Kato considered the answer for a while and nodded his head, satisfied; they were both similar in that way. 'Are the shi-kheu also *old ones*?' he asked.

'Not they, they have old ones and young ones, and they die, but they too live much longer than your kind.'

'What about your kind then? How many of you are there?' Kato asked.

'Hmmm…' Kene said. 'Not many, my little friend, and not nearly enough'.

'Why did Alhou make so few of you, Kene?' It seemed to him that the creator had been very uncaring of the timi-ala.

A bittersweet smile flitted across Kene's mouth momentarily. 'There were more of us, but in other places when the time came, our kind went for the *long sleep*. Now there are fewer than when we started out.'

'How do you know when it's time, Kene?'

'The *long sleep*?' Kato nodded. 'Something inside, a restlessness. It was put in us at the beginning and there is no need for any telling…' He paused. 'We just know.' He did not sound very sure.

For a long while neither of them spoke, and there was silence except for the hooting of owls and Kene's deep sighs.

'And now you know…' Kato whispered.

The giant considered something for a while and rumbled, 'Come. There is something I want to show you.' He stood up purposefully.

Kato raised an eyebrow and gave him a puzzled look.

Kene chuckled. 'Along with the stories and the adventures there are to be lessons.' He pulled him to his feet. 'And tonight is when we start.'

Kato placed his hands on his hips and looked up at the giant doubtfully. 'I don't like the idea. I get enough lessons from my parents and at the school.'

'You are a storyteller, not just any person. Surely you must understand that the listening is more important than the telling.'

Grudgingly Kato allowed the giant to put him on his shoulders. Without any warning at all Kene began a mighty sprint. Mercifully, Kato managed to secure a shaggy knot of the giant's hair. He knew that Kene wouldn't put him in danger and that he'd catch him even if he happened to lose his perch. Yet, that knowledge didn't make it any better. His teeth peeked out involuntarily a moment later as the wind whiffing past stoked a fiery thrill within him.

The vegetation gradually began to change with the terrain. The tall pines and straight firs gave way to shorter, wiry bushes. They reached a cluster of huge boulders, some so big that they could be a hill by themselves. Their pace slowed.

'What is this place?' Kato asked, his mouth open.

'A place lost to time,' Kene said. 'No human has been here for more than a thousand years.'

'A thousand years?' Kato cried as he scrambled down Kene's knees. The idea of so many years together boggled his mind. Kene walked towards the centre of the rock formations until soon a village came into view. Under the moonlight it looked eerie and strange. Very obviously deserted, there were broken pots strewn everywhere, and on drawing closer Kato saw that everything, including the houses, was made of mud.

'Where did they go?' Kato asked. Warily at first, he began to stroll through the village, peering around corners and tip-toeing across broken pottery.

'I do not know,' Kene replied. 'They left slowly, a few at a time, and one day there was no one left.'

The idea that people could simply leave altogether was very strange to Kato. The Sumi were an inquisitive people, often divvying up to form other villages elsewhere, but they never abandoned a village completely.

'Will we also disappear someday, Kene?' Kato asked, turning around, a cold realization slowly beginning to dawn on him.

'Your village will disappear someday,' Kene replied. 'The land has buried more villages than you can count.'

Kato imagined a time when the familiar winding path that led up to his village would reveal a barren slope instead of the huts that housed his villagers. Or maybe there would be other houses and another people. The thought drove a stab of ice through his heart.

'Nothing is immortal. Everything changes.'

'Even the mountains?' Kato asked, turning fully towards Kene. The ethereal moonlight glinted in the pools below Kene's heavy brows. He breathed in and out audibly for a while before nodding.

Kato closed his eyes slowly. The idea that a day would come when nothing he knew would remain filled him with sorrow. What would such a world look like? Would other people then pick through the ruins of his own world as he and Kene were doing now? Who would remember them?

'The stories, that is how we live. The greatest and the smallest of living things.'

Kato turned away to look at the ghostly ruins once more. A living village a thousand years ago stood in front of him, deserted and in shambles. A shiver suddenly ran up his exposed arms. He understood why Kene wanted a storyteller, but why him? *Why is Kene spending all this time telling a mute boy all of this?*

'Why me, Kene?' he asked glumly.

'What do you mean?' Kene asked.

'In case you haven't noticed yet, I'm a mute!' Kato snapped.

'Ah, I see what you mean.' Kene said, appearing to be considering the problem at hand. 'Two things I promise you, Kato,' he began, 'a story is more than just the telling of it. Secondly, if you learn everything I teach you, when it's time for me to go you will be, most definitely, a storyteller.'

Kato thought about it for a while and clicked his tongue. *Maybe he really could become a storyteller*. Tilting his head, he thought about what Kene's promise hinted at. The possibility of his deepest desire becoming reality filled him with both elation and dread. Quickly blinking the thought away, he left it just out of sight—close enough for comfort, yet far enough that the fear of disappointment wouldn't cause him too much anxiety. He wasn't going to ask the question straight. Giving Kene a guarded smile he nodded his head.

He went back to exploring the village. Pinching his nose shut, he peered into a hut. 'Don't go in,' Kene warned from a few huts behind. 'You don't know what's inside.'

The roof of the house had caved in and moonlight streamed in through a hole. Distracted by something, Kato barely heard Kene's warning.

'I think there are small puppies here,' he said as he crept in. 'No!' Kene shouted, and almost at the same time a furious, screeching devil made for him from the shadows. 'Aaaah!' Kato yelled and backpedalled as fast as he could, but the devil was too quick! There was nothing to do but wait for his death.

An overpowering smell filled his nostrils as the thing, whatever it was, flew at him like a demon! Completely helpless, he threw up his arms in front of his face, partially for defence but mostly so he wouldn't be able to see the monster. 'Ow!' Kato yelped in pain. Something had grabbed him by his arm and he was being hauled back through the air!

He braced himself for impact, fully expecting to be quashed like a dung beetle. To his overwhelming relief, he was quickly gathered under one of Kene's huge arms and carried away fast like a stolen chicken. When he'd had time to catch his breath, he looked back at the ghostly scene they'd left behind. Outlined in the moonlight he saw a shape standing on its hind legs at the village perimeter, and beside it three little busy shapes. He exhaled a big whoosh of air and shook his head with a grin. He was finally able to put everything together: the weird smell, the waddling shape, low to the ground, the screech. He'd come upon a mother hog badger with her pups.

When they were far enough Kene stopped running. Kato began to chuckle breathlessly, and a deep rumble began in Kene's chest too. Like corn popping in the fire it began—one here and another there almost bashfully, slowly building into a riot of rumbling and sniggering. They burst out laughing at the same time and Kene lowered Kato to the ground with unsteady hands as the laughter rocked his body. Kato rolled on the ground helplessly, thumping his chest again and again while Kene sat cross-legged and howled at the moon with tears streaming down his cheeks.

When he recovered sufficiently Kato looked at Kene who was curled up in a fetal position on the ground, rocking from side to side. A wide smile spread on his face. He felt for the first time since they'd met that Kene wasn't just a giant from the folk tales but a friend. The thought filled his chest with warmth.

'When will you visit me again?' Kato asked. They were sitting cross-legged, facing each other at the edge of his village. The terraced fields reflected the silver moonlight on their watery surfaces like many broken panes of glass. Somewhere south a jackal found something funny to cackle at.

'When the moon is nice and bright.'

'Why only when the moon is bright?' Kato complained.

Kene laughed. 'Your questions are as numerous as the stars, little man. Because unlike me you cannot see when it's dark.' He paused and spoke with something like regret, 'I can only lend you my speech, not my sight.'

'Oh, okay,' Kato mumbled, feeling a little gutted.

'Next time I'll take you to Lakhe and tell you a story, so cheer up, little man,' Kene said.

'What story, Kene?' Kato asked excitedly.

'Next time, next time,' Kene said like an exasperated old man. 'You must go home now, or you won't get any sleep at all,' he said, getting up and walking towards the village. Kato followed without protest. Imperceptibly a sleepiness descended on him like a heavy mist, and between one step and another he fell into a deep slumber that left him no time for anything resembling thought.

7

Amuhaqhi

JUNE

'Ishou.' Apu happily chomped on a boiled sweet potato produced from his satchel. Kato declined to share it with him fearing what other strange stuff he might have in there.

'How do you suppose the white man came to be so white?' he asked between munching. Kato huffed in annoyance. *As if I would know the answer to such a silly question*, he thought.

'You know what I think?' Apu lowered his voice conspiratorially. 'I think that when Alhou made men he made us Sumis in the summer sun, hence we are nice and brown, but the white men… he must have made them in the winter when the sun barely shines, hence they became pale and colourless!' He looked very proud at having answered a question that only he would ask.

Though Kato would never openly say it, for that would mean subjecting himself to endless self-important pronouncements, he did have to grudgingly admit that Apu did make a sort of sense. The idea that Alhou made men at different times, and in different seasons, seemed preposterous, but it was a fact that people came in different colours, like roast corn. He made a face, disliking the idea. The thought of the creator roasting people over a giant fireplace to differing degrees of *doneness* was too macabre. *Seasons then...* he thought. *Yes, seasons. He is quite clever.*

Spring had just arrived, and fresh green leaves had begun to appear on trees and vegetation. Before long, bright flowers would crown the trees and nature would go into a prolonged celebration. Spring in the Naga mountains isn't something polite and gentle. It isn't quaint and doesn't bashfully ask to be let in. No, it is instead like the relative that comes over once a year, knocks your door down and drinks all of your rice beer while telling you the most rib-tickling jokes. So riotous are the colours and scents that the waking daytimes leak into dreams, or maybe it's the other way around.

Yet, the colour didn't come alone. It was stalked by the gauntness of hunger. Most of the village folk would have come close to exhausting their grain accumulated from the last harvest. And like a cruel joke, while the birds let loose their euphonic arias, the hungry stomachs of the village folk sang their own sombre choruses. People lived in the halfway world of fantasy, wishing that July would come soon with corn and fruits.

Kato and Apu waded into the hip-high grass on the fields that had been left to rest for the year. The wind blew the sea of grass this way and then that way, like a great river hiding gigantic fishes in the swells and dips. Yelling and laughing they dove into the waves of green, fishermen of renown! The wind buffeted and carried their voices and shrieks so that it seemed as though there were many other ghostly children playing with them.

This had always been their playground, this openness and vastness. This was their haunt, their solace undisturbed. Here there was no need to hide, yet no one could find them either if they so desired. 'I'm the deer, ishou!' Apu yelled and ran. Needing no encouragement, Kato dashed after him down the slope, never sure where his next step was going to land, always one foot away from certain disaster!

He gulped air by the mouthful and looked at Apu who lay heaving on the ground, eyes closed, his face a very deep shade of red. Their unhinged laughter that had echoed over the mountainside just moments before ebbed into a low, stumbling hiccup. 'Heheh…heh…heh…' Apu sputtered as he sat up, wiping the sweat off his brows. Kato plonked down beside him, wheezing his queer laugh. Scraped elbows on bruised knees, they sat there on the grassy slope, looking into the horizon. Kato lay down on his back and inhaled deeply.

It had been more than ten days since Kene visited but this time there were no doubts. It had been no dream. *What an amazing being, the shi-kheu!* Kato thought, grinning from ear to ear. His breath had caught in his throat when the little figure first stepped out from the shadow of the trees. First he had been concerned for its safety, so vulnerable it had looked, but then the animals came, and in no time all his concerns vanished, replaced by awe. *So strange how things work,* he thought. *So many people in the world, and yet, it is I, a boy who cannot speak, that saw the shi-kheu!*

Recalling Kene's and his close escape in the deserted village, and the sounds of them howling at the moon, he fought off a bout of laughter and pretended to yawn instead. Apu would suspect something strange was up if he suddenly began laughing for no reason.

His mind drifted off after a while as he considered the shi-kheu once more. He'd heard about the aki-ghau, an ape-like spirit that used to guard the homes of people. It is said that they were seen weaving their way among the rafters of houses, but that had stopped years ago. For no obvious reason, people just stopped seeing them. *Chased away by half pants and gunshots.*

The sound of Apu singing jerked him back to the present. He looked at his friend as he sang a love song soulfully. Apu's voice had a tendency to crack every now and then and wasn't very suited to singing, but he made up for it with spirit. Kato nodded along and considered to himself the wonderful fact that he'd already spoken with Apu's voice twice. He felt a little guilty about it, as if he'd taken something from his friend without his permission. Normally he'd have a very hard time keeping anything from Apu, but quite perplexingly he didn't want to tell him about Kene at all. He knew it wasn't selfishness, but something to do with the person he was in his other life. Kene didn't know about the coward he harboured inside, and he was afraid that if Apu were to meet Kene, he'd find out from him. If the moon was any indication, Kene would be coming soon. He bristled with excitement.

With the slightly off-pitch, but strangely pleasing singing of Apu in the background Kato slipped away to the great forests and to the otherworldly view from Lakhe's height. There, he was more than the boy who *grunted like the beasts.* Yet there was no doubt that all of it would end soon; Kene had been very clear about that, about the *long sleep.* Would he have to return to being simply the mute boy once more? Did Kene's promise mean what he secretly hoped? He swallowed hard and turned sideways, hiding his face from Apu.

'Ishou, ishou!' He opened his eyes to find Apu shaking him. There was light rain splattering cold droplets on his face. One look at the quickly darkening sky told him that the drizzle would soon become a thunderstorm. Wasting no time, they ran as fast as their feet would carry them, but by the time they reached the village they were both thoroughly drenched.

'Like this.' Kene took the leaf from him and with a few folds it became a mountain. Kato marvelled at the dexterity of the giant fingers. It reminded him of his father's clever fingers, weaving bamboo into all kinds of things. He tried it again, and this time under Kene's close watch he too made his own mountain and placed it next to the two bigger ones. It occurred to him just then that Lakhe's leaves felt more like cloth than leaves. He plucked another big leaf and felt it in amazement.

'Tonight, I'll tell you about us—the *old ones*,' Kene said, interrupting his thoughts. 'What do you know of us?'

'I know what my mother told me.' Kato folded the leaf into a small square and tucked it under his thigh. 'Alhou created all things,' he began. He told Kene about how the creator made humans and animals. How the *old ones* were made to watch over the creator's work and how the timi-ala in particular were made for the welfare of humans. He realized that this was the first time he had told a story, and he felt elated.

'Hmmm...' Kene rumbled. 'A good story indeed, with one correction.'

Kato frowned in confusion. He'd heard the story countless times from his mother and his grandmother. How could there be anything to correct?

'We, the ones you call timi-ala, were never made to watch over your kind.' Kene paused. 'Yes, we did help your kind once in a while, but our purpose was to watch over the land.'

Kato balked. How could such a big detail have been wrong? He'd heard the story so many times that even now he felt as though it was Kene who was mistaken. Yet, it was *his* story. He knew it better than any human.

'Yes, there were others, spirits and the charmed, ones who followed your kind when you moved from place to place. But we the timi-ala were never supposed to move.'

'Why?' he asked.

'Come here,' Kene said, walking to Lakhe's trunk. Kato rose to his feet wordlessly and followed. 'Place your ears here,' the giant said, pointing at a spot.

Confused, Kato did as instructed. The bark felt warm despite the coolness of the night air. 'What am I supposed to hear?' he asked.

'Stop talking and concentrate,' Kene replied, almost curtly.

Exhaling in frustration Kato closed his eyes and tried to focus on whatever he was supposed to hear. At first he thought it was his own pulse but then it became obvious that another rhythm had begun pounding in his ear. With a depth that sounded limitless and cavernous this other rhythm beat once in the time his heart beat five times. The resonance of each beat so majestic that one beat seemed to continue where the other ended.

'That, my friend, is the heartbeat of the land,' Kene said, smiling.

'It is alive!' Kato said, his eyes flying open. 'Like a real person!'

Amusement danced in the big, luminescent pools of Kene's eyes. 'The land is the oldest and it is very much alive. It is the land that sustains everything that lives.'

'Why can I hear it through Lakhe?' Kato bent again to the trunk and listened to the great heartbeat.

'My sister's roots go very deep, right to the heart of the land.'

Kato lifted his head and rubbed his face furiously. This was really getting far too complicated for his little brain to understand. 'All this is good but weren't you going to tell me about the *old ones*, Kene?'

'My friend, the story of the land is the story of all of us. Listen now and remember well.'

Kato's ears immediately perked up. He could tell that a story was about to show itself.

'Before any of us, the land was made, and it was made so that it would be the giver of all life. And how should the land do so?'

Kato looked at Kene through squinted eyes but remained silent.

'Liking the story so far?' Kene asked and Kato nodded happily.

'The roots,' Kene continued. 'The land gives life through the roots.'

'Eh?' Kato interjected. 'What do you mean? Plants have roots, trees have roots. What about animals and men? What of you, *the old ones*?'

'It is simply a matter of looking but all of us have roots, from the greatest to the humblest. None of us can survive without the land.'

Kato scrunched his eyebrows and concentrated, trying to imagine him and Kene with roots. The thought was strange and disconcerting. He wanted to ask further but Kene quickly held up a hand.

'It is not a matter of questioning, Kato,' Kene said. 'When the sun disappears at dusk do you think it gone forever when it cannot be seen? No, you know that it will rise again in the morning. So also, though your roots might not be seen, believe me when I say that they are very much there.'

'Go on,' Kato said, a little doubtfully.

Kene tilted his head and smiled reassuringly. 'If you become a storyteller you will see for yourself, but for now, just trust me.'

'The trees and plants have roots already that reach into the ground. But everything else the land must sustain another way. How?'

Something struck Kato. Why was Kene telling him all this? He had an inkling that all of this led somewhere. He remembered a saying of his people. 'Our tribe says that a people without stories perish ... Are the stories how the land gives life to us?'

'Ah!' Kene said happily. 'The stories are indeed what keep our roots alive. But not every story though.'

'What do you mean?'

'Not every story is true, Kato,' Kene explained. 'Some are cooked up by people with vivid imaginations, others are complete lies.' Narrowing his eyes he leaned down and whispered forebodingly, 'Some are even told with evil designs.'

Kato nodded.

'But the stories that carry truth...' Kene's eyes became soft, brimful of something tender. 'These go deep into the land and draw forth life, feeding the roots that sustain us above.' He announced solemnly, 'If you are to be a storyteller you must be a truth teller, Kato. You must tell the truth unfailingly.'

Kato thought deeply before speaking up. 'Is that all there is to it?' he asked very seriously. 'If that is all I am quite sure that I can do it.'

Kene laughed. 'If you only knew what it takes to tell the truth you wouldn't think it so easy.' He said nothing for a while.

'But to answer your question, that isn't all there is to it,' he said, breaking the silence. 'Remember our deal?'

Kato nodded.

'It is not I but the land who will judge you.'

'I do not understand,' Kato said, furrowing his eyebrows.

'You must make with the land an unbreakable oath.' He raised an eyebrow and gave Kato a strange look, as though he expected a response.

'What?' Kato asked, feeling very confused.

Kene simply wriggled his eyebrows in response and waited. He finally threw his hands up and spoke a strange word in frustration. 'Your people, what is the strongest oath for your people?'

Kato hesitated for a short while, wondering what this had to do with everything. When it finally hit him his eyes went wide in shock. 'The oath we make by biting the earth!'

'Yes!' Kene said. 'How did you think your people started doing it in the first place? It was we that taught you.'

'Oh!' In a roundabout way, all of this began making sense to him.

'And just as death and misfortune befalls someone who lies under such an oath, a false oath made with the land ends in madness and then death,' Kene said ominously.

'I wouldn't make a false oath,' Kato said, half to himself. He didn't understand why one might make a false oath. The consequence was far too frightening. It was common knowledge amongst his people that an oath breaker would not be spared by the spirits.

'I am quite relieved that you should think so.' Kene's eyes twinkled.

'Who tells the stories for the animals?' Kato asked.

'The shi-kheu tells the story of the animals,' Kene answered. Kato nodded seriously. *Who else.*

'Now how about a story about myself?'

Kato clapped happily and made himself more comfortable, lying down sideways on the big logs.

'A very long time ago, before your people, the Sumis, ever came to be here, I roamed these great forests and mountains. I too was young then and restless of heart, though I'm sure you must find that hard to believe. Young, curious, and constantly in search of new things. Once, another timi-ala came into my territory and brought with him amazing stories—of lands where the ground is as flat as a plate as far as one can see, of mountains where nothing grew except a cold, white cotton, and of the oceans! We, the *old ones*, watch over the land but a few of us are also great wanderers, a very dangerous thing to do, I might add.'

'Why?' Kato asked curiously.

'Oh, it will make itself clear as my story goes on,' Kene dismissed his question with a casual wave.

'I was enchanted by his stories and by these wonderful places he spoke about, most of all by the ocean,' he continued. 'When he left in search of more places he gave me a conch. "Place your ear on the opening and you will hear the ocean," he said. Sure enough, when I placed my ear on the opening, I could hear the distant roaring of mighty waters.

'My heart became completely besotted with the idea of the ocean, until one day I bade farewell to sister tree and left in search of the ocean.'

Kato sat upright, transfixed by Kene's story.

'I walked and walked for many days, hundreds of days, across plains and mountains, across strange forests of rocks and boulders, across boiling streams black as soot, across the lands of men who rode buffaloes. But always, the conch would carry the ocean's voice to me, and I would move on.

'After many, many days of walking, I finally reached the ocean.'

'Whoa!' Kato exclaimed, hardly able to contain his excitement.

'It was many times more magnificent than I had imagined. Little friend, if you stood on the shore, you could not see any land for as far as your eyes can see. Only water, endless water,' Kene said wistfully. 'I stayed by the ocean for a long, long time, and there too I found another of my kind, but not the same. She was happy to have me with her, but often she would say, "You must return before long," and that irked me.'

'One day she asked me for my name and I found that I couldn't remember it. "You *must* return, or your roots will pull away completely," she said, and I became filled with unbearable sadness. All of a sudden, my heart desperately longed for the mountains and the forests, and sister tree. I looked and found the last remains of my roots, and so, leaving my companion and the conch that had lured me, I followed them back to my mountains.'

It was a good story but it left Kato feeling sad. 'Do you miss the ocean, Kene? Do you miss your companion?'

'Sometimes I do, but she is of the ocean, and I am of the mountain,' he replied with a heavy sigh.

They sat there in silence, until again a heavy sleepiness came over Kato, and before he could fall onto the platform Kene's giant arms cradled him safely.

8

Aniqhi

JULY

Kato hurled his satchel onto his bed, dashed into the kitchen for a drink of water and was halfway into a sprint when his mother called from the garden, 'Ilomi, how was school?'

He groaned with impatience but stopped. He and Apu were to meet for some mischief making. Walking over to the garden, he saw her busy amongst the little onion shoots. She smiled at him and asked about school again. He placed two fingers against his forehead and grunted.

'That's good,' she stood up, clapping her hands to rid them of the dark soil.

'Ilomi…' she began. He closed his eyes and exhaled mournfully. He knew that voice.

'Will you be a darling and do something for me?'

'Ilomi, please.' She stood before him, pleading with that look he knew so well.

He just sat on the bench, looking away. He didn't like it one bit. If he'd known that this was what she wanted he'd have just sped away when she called.

'He is your uncle,' she said, kneeling down. He turned his eyes away. 'I know they aren't kind to you.' He felt her hand pulling his face to meet her eyes. 'We cannot only be kind to those who are kind to us, my love.'

Why not? he asked moodily, touching both shoulders one after the other with his right thumb. His uncle and aunt had never wasted any opportunity to make him feel bad. 'We lose nothing by being kind,' she smiled at him. He looked at her beautiful face sullenly.

'For my sake?'

He finally let a smile through and stood up.

Her laugh tinkled in the afternoon air, and she hugged him. 'You're a very good boy.'

Rolling his eyes he took the basket of vegetables from her hand, quickly gave her a kiss, and ran away.

⸺

Kato dipped under a bush when he heard voices. If he wasn't on his errand, he would have taken the path around the village to get to Apu's house. He waited until they had passed.

Just leave the basket outside their door and leave silently—that was the plan until he peered out from behind a tree where the path bent. His aunt was sitting outside her house! Kato felt annoyance rise inside him. The only reason he'd agreed was because at midday most villagers would be working in the fields or their garden, and he could have done the errand unnoticed. He glared angrily at the basket in his hands and felt very tempted to just leave it there. But he couldn't because he'd promised to do so for her sake. He leaned back into the shade and thought about his situation.

He'd just promised to give it to them, not hand it over personally. There was no way he was going to walk up to their house just like that now. He mulled over his options and finally made up his mind.

Retracing his steps, he dropped below a hedge and slowly crept into someone else's courtyard. Sumi homes mostly have only a bush or a hedge to demarcate boundaries, and so he planned to circumvent his problem by coming around instead of to the front. He was going to leave the basket in their backyard. Hoping that no one would see him and mistake him for a thief, he quickly slid into the shadows.

He reached his uncle's backyard without any difficulty. Making sure that there was no one around, he slowly crept into their garden. Lowering himself amongst the plants he proceeded as inconspicuously as he could manage.

Snort! Snort! One of his uncle's fat pigs lumbered up, noticing a stranger in their domain. Soon the whole gang began making a huge commotion. He dropped down on the ground and held his breath. The blood pounded in his ears. 'Husband!' he heard his aunt yell from the courtyard. 'Check on the pigs!'

'What?' his uncle shouted from inside.

'The pigs!' she yelled back.

He heard a door creak and decided not to wait any longer. His mother would have to be satisfied with this. Standing up to his full height he tossed the basket of vegetables as far as he could towards the house. Without stopping to check where it had fallen, he made a mad dash out of there.

'Hey mute!'

Kato continued walking with a grimace.

'*Hoi!* Are you deaf too, you idiot?'

Kato kept walking. This wasn't the first time Yemishe had picked on him, and ignoring him would make him move onto another victim, someone easier. He quickened his pace, hoping to reach the small diversion that led into the trees where he could sprint away, leaving the savages behind.

'Where's the rat that follows you around, idiot?' Yemishe had caught up and was now walking behind him with his three lackeys, shouting in his ears. 'Must think yourself very grand for what you did the other day, no?'

Kato gritted his teeth but kept walking.

'Maybe he's also deaf, Yemishe,' Atopu, the sneaky one, said with a sneer. The truth was that it was he who controlled the bigger boy with his cunning suggestions and crafty insinuations.

Running out of taunts, the bully took a long pause, reaching for the most hurtful thing he could find. 'Were you born an idiot because your mother lay with Izheshe?'

A stunned silence followed. Kato stopped walking.

'Amu Yemishe, I think someone's coming,' Ilhopu, the youngest of the lackeys, punctured the silence, anxiety threading through his voice. 'Let's just go.'

'Shut up, you buffoon! If you lack the guts, go!' Kato heard Ilhopu stammer and run off.

'Did your mother lie with Izheshe, you idiot?' Yemishe repeated.

Kato felt suffocated by the rage inside. Yemishe had accused his mother of committing adultery with Izheshe, the village idiot who drooled and ran around naked, sometimes covered in his own filth. Normally, Kato would have walked on silently, but the dishonour to his mother he would not tolerate. His body trembled in anticipation of the rage that was making its way to the surface. The hair on his arms stood up, and a stinging heat began to gather behind his neck and ears. He turned around and faced the accuser, sense and reason quickly draining away bit by bit. He would make him pay.

Yemishe stepped back and so did his remaining lackeys. It was supposed to end with Kato fumbling and running away in tears, not this spectre of rage and ferocity. Kato took a heavy step towards them, fists balled so tight they looked white, the exhalation of his breath hot against his lips.

He could see the fear in their eyes. They'd mistaken his evasions for fear. They did not scare him. They did not know of the tiger he rode: the other side of his terror that knew neither reason nor caution.

'What are you boys up to?' the stern voice of their teacher interrupted, seconds before the sequence culminated in violence.

Yemishe and the two lackeys spun around and ran.

'Were they giving you a hard time, Kato?' the teacher asked.

'Quite fortuitous that I happened to be passing by,' he said to himself when Kato didn't respond.

Kato let himself regain his composure before finally shaking his head.

'If you say so,' the teacher said sadly. 'Go on home now, and make sure that Apu comes to class tomorrow. That boy will use any excuse to escape school,' he said with a wry smile and walked on uphill.

Exhaling slowly Kato unclenched his fists and felt blood rush back into them like little needles. Even he was surprised by the taste of corroded iron in his mouth, and the ground was stained with flecks of pink when he spat on it.

'We better leg it, ishou.' Apu stood up, casting a worried look at the busy-looking clouds. Kato shared his concern. The prospect of getting wet wasn't what worried them but the fact that they were supposed to be grazing Apu's parents' long-haired goats. They'd left them grazing on a broad hillside and usually they'd be fine by themselves until the boys got back. But the problem was that goats absolutely hate rain and if it started pouring there was no telling where the animals would go in search of shade.

Thankfully they found the animals still loitering about uncomfortably when they reached the hillside. The promised downpour graciously held itself back until they reached the village and though wet, they weren't completely drenched.

'There you go!' Apu exclaimed, pushing the last goat into the enclosure. Kato leaned back, hands on hips, and heaved a sigh of relief.

'You hear that, ishou?' Apu asked, perking his ears.

Kato could make out the low murmuring of several male voices from inside Apu's kitchen. They looked at each other with huge grins at the same time. This was a sound they were very familiar with, the harbinger of those most delectable things—stories! His day, soured by Yemishe and his lackeys, was beginning to look more promising. Silently they slunk into the kitchen.

'Here, here,' Apu's mother gestured urgently to them from the hearthside. They crept to her and sat cross-legged on the warm mud floor. Kato spotted his father amongst the small group of men assembled on the wooden platform near the window. A fantastic breeze was lavishing its attention on those inside. It opened onto the whole eastern side of the mountains and made for a fantastic view that he'd always envied; their own kitchen window opened towards their neighbour's garden. His father made eye contact with him, and he nodded with a wry smile.

Apu's mother ladled hot, sticky corn soup, seasoned with just a little salt and ausu, a close cousin of the common ginger, into two bowls. Kato took it gratefully and blew into the bowl, eyes fixed on the group of men.

'Your father saw a leopard carrying away one of our pigs!' she whispered urgently as she tussled her son's hair.

Whoa! That was news indeed! Kato thought.

'A big one with a limp. He said its spots made it look like a python when it moved in the sunlight! By our garden, carried it off as easily as you please!'

Surely an injured leopard that can no longer hunt in the wild... Kato thought. Such an animal posed great danger to the village, for a predator would always want the killing—want to sink its fangs in warm blood. No injury would make it start eating grass and leftovers. And which creature in nature is as helpless as human children? The thrill of the potential danger made him smile.

'No, I'm serious,' Jekishe, the man with a missing thumb, said. He'd lost it while he was whittling on a bamboo with a dao that was much too sharp. 'Men do get ripe sometimes,' he continued. The other men harrumphed in disbelief, but he continued.

'Let me tell you the story of a great uncle. This was before we were even born, you follow?' The other men quieted down for if his theory involved a story, that too of a relative, things could become a lot more plausible. And just the thought of a man ripening was so macabre that it shushed them down. Kato slowly brought a steaming spoonful of the soup to his lips and slurped carefully. The salt in the soup made the cut in his tongue sing with pain and he quickly moved the broth to the other side of his mouth.

'So then,' Jekishe went on, 'this great uncle was newly married, and his wife was with child. They were happy and content, for what worry should a young couple with a field full of ripening grain and a baby on the way have?' The other men nodded their heads in agreement.

'Ah! To be young and hopeful!' Futhena, the oldest in the group, exclaimed with a wistful look.

'Anyway, as I was saying,' the storyteller continued, looking a little sour at being interrupted, 'everything was perfect until one day my great uncle began to smell sweet.'

'Sweet? What sort of thing is that?' Apu's father interjected with an annoyed look, probably thinking that they were being told a tall tale. Quite ironic, really, with *his* record, Kato thought with a grin.

With the suddenness of a hiccup, it began to pour outside, and Jekishe raised his voice to be heard.

'Now look,' the storyteller retorted angrily, 'I'm just telling you what my grandmother told me.' This seemed to pacify Apu's father who grudgingly motioned at him to continue.

'Since I wasn't there myself, I couldn't describe it exactly, but my grandmother said that he began to smell like berries or fruits do when they are ripening. Sweet, you know…' he added as an explanation. The men collectively scrunched their foreheads, trying to imagine a man who smelled like a ripe fruit, and from the looks on their faces they didn't like it at all. Kato was much better at this than other people, and when he focused his mind on the idea, the smell that filled the space between his brow almost made him retch. The downpour became a torrent, and the storyteller was all but shouting now.

'First it was just a faint smell, but soon it became such a reek that even his wife couldn't stand to be with him for long. Naturally they were very disturbed and did everything they could to wash the smell off. Bathing in ashes, standing over smoke until he couldn't breathe, swimming in the river until his skin became wrinkly like an old man's—nothing worked. No matter what they tried he still reeked.'

'Eeeeeesh!' old man Futhena grimaced.

The storyteller nodded in agreement. 'As you can imagine, it became unbearable. So unbearable indeed that they paid a visit to the Tu-umi woman of the village, hoping that she would be able to help. But alas! No help awaited them there. Instead, she told them that something horrible was happening to him—he was getting ripe. When the time reached its fullness, the tigers would come to devour his ripe flesh. She could not help at all but advised him to stay indoors and board up his house so the tigers wouldn't be able to get at him. The ripening would last for a certain period and if his death could be prevented, it would go away.'

Kato glanced at Apu in horror and found him equally alarmed.

Jekishe nodded, confirming their darkest misgivings. 'For ten days his clan waited guard outside his house, and for ten days the tigers would appear to take him. But each time they were thwarted by the spears and the daos of his kinsmen. On the eleventh day the tigers didn't come, and so the clan, exhausted by the vigil, left thinking it was over. His wife pleaded with them to stay, for the sweet smell was still on him, but they left. On the twelfth night the tigers came and tore down the bamboo walls of his home and dragged him screaming horribly into the forest. Not even his bones could be found.' And thus he ended the macabre story.

Everyone was utterly speechless. That such a thing could even be possible! The rain that had begun suddenly was petering out already, but the muted greyness still remained outside. The blazing kitchen fire happily took centre stage, casting its orange glow on the aghast faces of everyone gathered there.

'So, what caused him to become ripe then?' Apu's mother asked from the fireside, breaking the thrall.

'Who knows… who knows indeed, and to think that tigers and men were brothers once…' Jekishe trailed off.

Kato found the story extremely disturbing. It seemed like the most unfair thing ever. It was bad enough that a man could become ripe, but to not even know why meant that it could happen to anyone! For who can protect himself from something he doesn't understand? He remembered Kene's story about the ocean and wondered how much of the world would remain unknown and unknowable even if one were to live several hundred years. The incurable curiosity he'd always held within drooped at the thought. He wanted to know everything there was to know!

'Ishou, what would you do if the leopard sprang down right in front of you while you were out walking?' They were outside sitting on the damp bamboo platform, cheerily chomping on roast buffalo skin. Kato grinned at his friend, showing teeth stained brown from burnt buffalo skin. Swiftly he leapt on Apu, and soon had him pinned, the little fellow unable to put up much of a struggle. They giggled and hollered so loudly that Apu's mother finally had enough and ordered them to go play somewhere else.

'But really, we need weapons, my dear fellow,' Apu said. Kato nodded furiously. This was a grand idea indeed! Weapons then, for two leopard slayers!

They laboured till evening with wood and dao in Apu's backyard, until finally their efforts birthed two substantial-looking clubs that were as ugly as they would be ineffective. Kato swung his club awkwardly. They were heavy, misshapen and very unwieldy but to his eyes they looked like the perfect weapons for renowned leopard slayers.

The setting sun and a growling stomach finally convinced Kato that it was time to go, and though Apu tried to wheedle him into staying for dinner, he made for home, club in hand, glancing uneasily at the bushes on the way. Apu would never know that he worked himself up into such a state of terror that he finally ran home howling, his club all but forgotten as it jangled on his shoulder.

Kato lay on his side rubbing his satisfied tummy languidly. After a delicious dinner of river crabs cooked in spicy bamboo shoot and wild leaves, he was peering at the night sky through the half-shut kitchen door. The moon was still a very thin sickle. Groaning impatiently, he wondered how many more days it would take for it to grow full and round. Kene would come to get him again, and with him would come a new adventure!

He heard his parents talking in hushed whispers outside. His eyes followed the orange light of the lamp in the darkness through the little gaps in the thatch. 'Ilomi, are you sure that we don't need to add another one?' his worried-sounding mother asked. 'Should do, should do…' his father replied, sounding unlike his usual self-assured self. 'Unless this one can use his hands like us…' he added ominously. 'Don't say such things!' his mother said, horrified, and quickly hushed her voice again. All this hush-hush, clandestine prowling made Kato feel as though the leopard were not an animal but some evil spirit prowling about in the dark, scheming to do harm to the villagers. He placed his hand on his heart and felt it beating furiously underneath.

His parents were checking on the pigs inside their makeshift shelter. They shuffled into the kitchen moments later and his father placed a stout stick against the door. Remembering his father's words about the leopard having hands like men, he felt a shiver climb his spine. Though he was terrified out of his wits he couldn't keep the excitement away.

9

The Hunt

Two days after the first sighting the leopard was spotted again. This time it was a graver incident for it had been stalking a child when the mother caught sight of it and scared it away with shouts and banging utensils. There was no doubt about it—a wounded leopard had staked out the village as its ground for easy pickings. There were enough stories about leopards and tigers dragging sleeping people out of their beds, and no one felt safe.

A hurried meeting was convened at the chief's house where all the men were summoned. After they came out the hunt was announced. It would be on the third day, as very serious preparations would have to be made for such a dangerous quarry. Till then, children were always to be accompanied by adults when outside, and school was called off.

=

'Just come in, ilomi,' Kato's mother called from the kitchen.

Casting an annoyed look in her direction he continued pacing the courtyard. The day of the hunt was here, and he hadn't slept a wink because of all the excitement!

His father had left before dawn after a great deal of sharpening and re-sharpening his spear blade. Kato had sullenly watched him work, nursing a great sense of injustice like an aggrieved mother. Only those who were sixteen and older, adult men in other words, could join in the hunting of big cats. He thought of some sixteen-year-old boys in his village and gritted his teeth. He was taller and stronger than most of them. But three years, merely *three* miserable years separated him from them! He walked with a timi-ala, had seen things that none of the villagers had, been on adventures that would make all of them gawk in wonder. Yet, he would not be allowed to join the hunt.

All he could do now was pace around like a headless chicken. His anger gave way to a moody resignation, and he dropped down on his parents' gazing bench. He saw people buzzing around further uphill through the gaps in the tree lines, busy with something or the other. Perhaps it was owing to his lack of sleep, which had left him in a lightheaded state, but there seemed to be an abnormal sharpness to everything this morning. It was as though everyone was part of a giant play, even the dogs and animals, but no one knew how it ended which drove them a little crazy.

Even now the distant baying of the hunting dogs, the shihatsu, with their cropped ears and docked tails, travelled to his ears with ominous significance. Somewhere in the forest was a leopard with a limp that was dropping its scent like offerings for the dogs.

The ancient ritual of the hunter and the hunted was about to begin—its edge as keen as that of a knife.

Kato could hear Shihato, the chief's black hound, crying like a banshee as he reared to get away from his owner and go tearing for the kill. The hunting dogs of the Sumis were a fierce type who bayed both wild boars and big cats, and among them Shihato was king. Smaller than average, he was a dog who made up in heart and grit what he lacked in size. He was such an excellent dog that people from other villages brought their female dogs to breed with him. Often, he'd hunt alone in the forest and bring dead game to his master, with not a single bite for himself.

In a moment, the scouting party was off! Kato shifted his weight on the bench to sit up. Closing his eyes, he tilted an ear towards the sound and moved his hand about as he tracked their movement in his head. He knew exactly what would happen. The dogs would lead their masters to the quarry, who'd then send word to the village men. The men would then circle the location of the leopard, beating drums and utensils—anything that made a noise—and woven bamboo walls, until the leopard was cornered in a small space. Finally, they'd close in on their quarry, using their long spears to kill it. A leopard was not something to be fought but trapped.

This method of hunting, though effective, wasn't without its dangers. Many times, the wild animal would break from cover, and charge the men while their trap was not yet sprung. Limbs and lives could be lost, and they had been on several instances.

After a while the sounds receded completely. Kato lowered his hands dejectedly and opened his eyes. All he could do now was hang around the stragglers, the old folk, women and children, far away from the action, and hope to deduce the tenor of the hunt from the sounds he heard. His anger returning, he slapped his thighs and stood up to go in.

≡

Inside, he found his mother busily pouring rice beer into long bamboo flutes. Later she'd wrap sticky rice, pork slow-cooked in its own juices, boiled bitter bulbs, and a spicy ginger paste, in banana leaves. There'd be one each for all three of them, and a few extra for friends and family who'd forgotten to bring their lunches to the hunt.

Still disgruntled, he made sure his mother could sense his displeasure by glowering in the doorway. She grinned at him.

'Hey little squirrel, come and help me.'

Unimpressed by this ploy to distract him, he huffed and stomped back out into the courtyard. He heard her laughing from the kitchen, which inflamed him so much that he kicked at a brinjal plant, making one of the bulbs fly. He felt sorry immediately after. A little mollified, he sat on the bench and wondered what his father might be doing now.

He was still brooding when Apu peeked out from the corner of the house.

'Whoooo! The hunt is on, ishou!' he exclaimed, flailing his hands in what he obviously thought was a good imitation of a spear throw, but he really just looked like a constipated crab.

Kato glared at him, which stopped the pendulous creature in his tracks.

Adopting a fatherly tone, Apu began, 'Now, now. I know it isn't fair but...' He let the sentence hang in the air and spread his hands in a gesture of helplessness. The stupid mimicry of the chief was so good that Kato chortled despite himself.

'Heh! Got you!' he said, punching Kato's shoulder and plopping down beside him without any invitation.

He tried not to give Apu the satisfaction of seeing him laugh, trying really hard to contain his bubbling mirth inside, but it only made matters worse. His treacherous mouth threatened to split into a wide smile. *No!* He was not going to let anything budge him from his high place of discontent!

'Anyway, what are you having for lunch later?' his impish friend asked, hushing his voice so it was only a whisper. 'My folks are having pumpkin!' he said, adding a 'Yechhh!'

The imp was here to wheedle food out of his mother! Despite his determination, Kato felt his righteous walls of discontent falter and he began to guffaw uproariously. Apu grinned at him, and a moment later joined in with the most shameless free-spiritedness.

'*Ah! This friend of mine!*' Kato thought a good five minutes later. '*What wrong did I commit to deserve him.*'

Looking sideways at his friend rubbing his aching tummy, he smiled fondly.

'Coming?' old Futhena's wife asked as she and her husband walked past.

'Waiting for Iza. Go on, we'll catch up soon,' Kato's mother informed her pleasantly.

Kato looked at all the people heading down towards the village gate and stamped his feet impatiently. Grunting with frustration he smacked a fist into the palm of the other hand. He knew his grandmother wasn't as quick as him, but he wished that for just today she'd hurry herself. Catching sight of her at last he raced up the path.

Before she had time to say anything he grabbed the basket in her hands and slung it on himself. 'Impatient, are we?' she chuckled. Taking her hand in his own he began walking to his mother who stood laughing, finding something about him funny.

They heard the assembly of people before they saw them. They were camped beyond the gates on an open slope that had trees running on its western flank. Interspersed with bushes and trees here and there for shade, it made the perfect picnic spot. Kato spotted the four-legged platform standing amidst the melee of people and his heart skipped a beat. After the hunt, *if* the leopard was killed, its carcass would be placed on the platform and a celebration would ensue. He became aware for the first time that this hunt was about the taking of life—whether it would be the leopard or a man, yet unknown. He swallowed slowly and hoped that the men would be okay.

The entire village was gathered here today, all 143 houses, and the gaggle of children made a sound that was almost as terrifying as the chanting of the menfolk. Even for Kato's village, an event of this scale was rare. People did go on hunts alone and in small groups, but for the whole village to turn out, exceptional circumstances were required, like a communal fishing expedition which happened around once in two years, or a situation like today's, involving rogue tigers, boars or leopards.

The men could be heard chanting their pentatonic *ho-he, ho-he* towards where the bamboos grew. Like an ominous refrain, the gongs and drums and the slapping of hide shields on bare thighs thundered in the background. Kato could only prowl about in frustration as the chanting, drumming and clanging continued to rise higher and higher. *They're getting close!* He winced helplessly. His mother was spooling cotton on her thighs from a basket, humming a song, no hint to suggest a wild animal prowling at the edges of the village. His grandmother spread a shawl on the ground and beckoned him to come sit by her.

Invisible to anyone else, a fierce struggle began within him. A foil to his paralyzing fear, there was a *need* in him to rush headlong into danger, a need that would punish him for days on end, whispering its accusations, *coward, idiot...* if he refused to give in.

He stood up quickly and prepared to leave.

'Where are you going?' his mother asked, looking up. Her restless eyes revealed the truth she was trying to hide behind her humming and busyness.

Not wanting to alarm her any further he signalled that he was going to find Apu.

'Do not wander into the forest,' she warned him. He nodded and turned to go but she grabbed at his hands furtively and made him look at her. 'Don't do anything foolish!'

He nodded and went on, guilt weighing him down. He *had* told her the truth. He *was* going to find Apu, but he also planned to slip away into the forest to watch the hunt, *with or without his friend*. She would have lost her mind if she knew.

Apu was raising a storm when Kato found him. Surrounded by a group of younger children, he was acting the part of both the leopard and the mighty warrior who would slay it. He was a great favourite of the younger children.

Spotting Kato, he abruptly brought his play to a close with a skewered leopard and a jubilant warrior all in a matter of a few heartbeats. Feeling cheated, the children protested.

'Amu Apu! Do it again! Do it again!' one boy shouted, with the others joining the chorus.

Acting important Apu strutted and preened. 'Now, now, children,' he began. Kato grinned at his friend's theatrics. 'I have grown-up stuff to take care of.'

Despite their protestations he walked over to his friend.

'The children, they adore m...' Before he could complete his sentence his friend dragged him away by the elbows.

'What in all my short, sweet life, Kato!' his horrified friend cried, after Kato conveyed to him his intent using a great many signs and pointing.

He was immediately pinched and motioned to lower his voice.

Apu continued in an incredulous whisper, 'I always knew you were strange in the head, but *this*!'

Kato simply stood with his chin jutting out and his gaze fixed squarely on Apu's eyeballs.

'Curse me!' Apu whispered, shaking his head and slapping his own face. Kato grinned like a sloth. He had him! Apu always slapped his own face when he was working up the courage to do something he knew he shouldn't.

Kato motioned for his friend to stop his terrified mutterings as they crouched in the low-growing foliage, a little to the west of the hunting ground. Getting past the camping group had been easy work for two young boys with plenty of experience in slinking around. Apu was still trying to get his friend to call off this madness. 'Ishou!' he whispered desperately. 'Let's just wait with the others!' It was to no avail for Kato's mind had been made.

'O mother!' Apu kept repeating, yet he stuck with Kato every step of the way. 'Here, let's wait here,' he whispered urgently, but they were still within earshot of the women and children, and Kato had no interest in stopping there. 'Curse me! Are you planning to lead us to the leopard's maws?' Apu said, eyes darting frantically in all directions.

Nearing a cluster of thickets, Kato held up a hand and dropped to the ground silently. Breathlessly, Apu sank down, and immediately began to burrow his way into the foliage. *That might not be a bad idea*, Kato thought, joining Apu. This was as close as even he dared to go, a stone's throw away from where the action was focused. In no time they were hidden inside the shrubs.

Kato felt Apu's hand gripping his arm hard. His friend was sweating profusely, and a trickle of sweat rolled down his skin where he touched him. Pressed on all sides by leaves, their hot breaths made the small space unbearably warm, but it was too late to look for another place. 'What a fool I am,' Apu exhaled mournfully, 'letting you drag me to my death.' Kato shook him to keep quiet. Ignoring the heat and his friend's chattering, he focused all his senses on the sounds of the hunting party. The voices of the men were clear, but his heartbeat thundered into his ears like the roaring of mighty waters, much louder than the banging skin drums of the hunters. Swallowing hard, he realized that while the excitement was still there, fear and anxiety had wrested firm control.

Looking at his quavering friend, Kato thought to himself that it would have been better to spare him this ordeal.

They crouched there, knees in the dirt, legs aching. The sounds of the hunt began to close in on a particular spot, the dogs getting more agitated and the drumming rising to a feverish pitch. The leopard had probably been sighted.

'Chou! Chou! He is off that way, Xusheto!' Kato heard Khaolipu's father shout, excitement and terror threading his voice.

Kato gripped one of Apu's sweaty arms so hard that his friend let out a small '*ow*'. It was beginning!

'That way! That way!' several voices joined together, panicked, their former bravado all but gone.

Next came the unhinged sounds of the dogs baying and the leopard snarling fearsomely. A dog went from barking to yelping to crying piteously, amplifying the howling of the other dogs. It had turned into utter chaos in a matter of seconds. Soon, it would be decided.

'He got Nitsuli! Damned bastard got my dog!' Phusheto exclaimed balefully.

'He's going to leap out of our circle! Watch out! He'll be gone into the forest if we let him!' a man screamed, voice distorted by panic.

'Aish! Khuzheto! Use your spear to push it back!' the chief shouted angrily.

'Why don't you do it!' Khuzheto answered back, just as angry.

The snarling leopard was creating havoc among the men, and all pretences at an orderly snare were being discarded hastily as dogs and men alike flew all over the forest floor, crashing through the undergrowth and into each other. Kato fought the urge to slip out of the bush for a better look. The tension was reaching its peak, like a bent bamboo tree just before it goes *crack*! Telling himself that it wasn't worth the risk he clenched his jaw and sat on the ground to relieve his thighs that were about to cramp.

Suddenly there was a shift, and the uproar headed in their direction! He looked at Apu and found his friend chattering like a senile ape. He debated whether to stay or go. The sound of bodies crashing through foliage and shrubs became louder and discernibly closer. He decided to risk discovery and leave the place. Grabbing Apu by the arm he began to creep back when suddenly the leopard burst into their cover.

Terrified, he fell back through the foliage with Apu onto the small clearing behind. Too afraid to take his eyes off the leopard, he hit the ground hard. Blood began to mix with dusty sweat on his bruised limbs. He tasted sand and grit in his mouth. The leopard emerged from their hiding place looking like something from his nightmares. It was as big as a calf and growled menacingly. Apu was frozen, muttering something indecipherable. Kato quickly took hold of his friend's sling bag and pulled him as far back as his strength would allow. He hoped to get Apu up and make a run for it if possible. But a great cat is no human. Within the blink of an eye, in one single terrifying bound, the leopard was within touching distance.

Apu whimpered and turned his eyes away. Kato could only watch, hypnotized by the leopard, its raging eyes, and the mesmerizing spots that rode its skin every time a muscle twitched. A serpentine tail flicked above its coiled torso, urgent and taut with terrible violence. Baring giant fangs it snarled in rage, maddened by its wound—a nasty gash on its hind leg. Oddly resembling a housecat in that moment, it lifted a paw armed with vicious claws, and tensed to strike.

Kato closed his eyes and waited for his death, his only thought being regret for forcing Apu to come on this suicidal mission. He reached out and, finding his shivering little friend, pulled him into his arms, shielding him with his body. Turning his head away from the oncoming assault, he waited. *Iza!* The thought sprang to life, urgent and desperate. 'Ishou, we're done,' Apu stated resignedly, at the end of one long, defeated exhalation of air.

When the hurricane of claws and teeth failed to come, Kato opened his eyes. The leopard stood with a baffled expression, sniffing furiously, its long whiskers probing the air for something. It ambled slowly to Kato and began sniffing at his face, its hot, rancid breath making his eyes tear.

It was at this moment that the men burst into the clearing. Kato heard them but couldn't look away from the hypnotic eyes, blazing with amber-coloured stars and stained with flecks of raging red. Apu made a sound like someone who was just waking up from a tortured sleep.

'Wait!' the chief bellowed. 'They're too close!'

'Let me.' It was his father.

In a matter of one single heartbeat, he watched the leopard take the impact of a spear in its side. *The heart.* The animal staggered and dropped to the ground, eyes still fixed on him. Kato held his breath and stared at the great amber eyes. The rage in them cooled as he watched, to be replaced by a look of vague surprise, soon replaced by confusion and fatigue. When the life finally flickered out, Kato drew in a shuddering, deep breath, and closed his eyes once more.

10

The Reckoning

Kato and Apu found themselves yanked up by the arms.

'Have you two lost your minds!' a voice demanded angrily.

'Dung for brains!' another voice followed.

'Now you'll get it, stupid disobedient children!' still another voice shouted.

Kato recognized Apu's father among the voices, but he couldn't tell which one it was. His mind was overwhelmed by the silence of his father and the shame that had begun to bloom in his ears.

The men circled them and continued to scold them angrily.

'Enough!' the chief said as he stepped forward. He gave them a very stern stare. 'Bind their hands and take them to the council hall. I'll deal with them later.'

Their hands were bound with some creepers, and as they were led away Kato saw his father's tired eyes, and he began to drown in a sea of shame. He felt his friend shiver uncontrollably, and he realized that he too was shivering. Some men lashed the leopard's carcass to a stout bamboo and off they went—*ho ho ho hoi.*

On the way to the council hall, they crossed the other villagers, and Kato looked down shamefacedly when he saw his stricken mother.

'What have you done, you fool!' Apu's mother shouted as she ran to her son and began pawing at his face, making him cringe in embarrassment. Soon she began to blabber and cry.

'Hush, woman!' her husband thundered. 'It's enough that our son has dung for brains. Don't you start with your antics now!' She sniffled and made even more pitiable sounds.

=

'Stay here, and don't try to go anywhere or it'll go worse for you,' Ato said, crouching down. Ato was a young man, around seventeen, and he'd always been kind to the both of them. 'You shouldn't have disobeyed the law, you know. But it's okay,' he added, trying to cheer them up a little. 'Despite his gruff ways, the chief has a kind heart, and though your actions will be punished you needn't fear too much.

'I'm off now! They'll be starting the dance soon,' he said, standing up, and then he was off racing down the sloping steps, whooping in excitement.

Kato peered around the council hall curiously. Despite the mess they were in this was the only chance they'd have to survey its insides until they became grown men themselves. It appeared to be simply another regular room. There was a fireplace in the centre and benches along all its sides. The only sign that matters of importance were discussed here was the absence of any windows. While the roof was designed to allow smoke to escape, and the woven thatch itself partially allowed air through, the absence of windows was telling in the soot-blackened hay.

'Well then, ishou, I suppose we're truly in it now!' Apu said, nudging his sides with his painfully sharp elbows. Kato drew in an asthmatic breath and exhaled jerkily. He had neither the strength nor the spirit to respond. He retraced his steps until he came to the moment on the slope when he'd lied to his mother. *Why do I have to be this way?* As far back as he could remember he'd had this rabid curiosity that refused to go away or be subdued. In the past too it had gotten him in trouble, like the time he'd let a new hen run away from its basket just because he wanted to know how they laid eggs. Today it had nearly cost Apu and him their lives.

He looked outside and noticed the daylight beginning to fade. *Won't be long*, he thought with a sinking heart.

'But that was the most dangerous situation we've ever been in, no Ishou? If only we had our clubs with us…' Apu blurted out excitedly after a while. There really was no keeping him down…

They filed in silently, all looking grim and serious. Only men could come to the council hall, and it looked like most of the village's menfolk had turned up. Many of them bore marks and scratches on their bodies from the hunt. The fatigue of the hunt and the leftover exuberance from the merrymaking made their bodies glint in the firelight. Both their fathers were there, and Kato baulked at the sadness he saw in his father's eyes. Apu's father knocked his son on the head angrily before taking his place on a bench.

The chief glowered at them.

'Laws are laws for a reason,' he began firmly, but not unkindly. 'Our forefathers had very good reasons for every law that exists today. Now I know how it might seem unfair to boys your age that you should be excluded from the hunt but there is something you must learn: you cannot act as you wish simply because you want to. Obeying the laws isn't just about doing what your elders tell you. No, it is about understanding who we are and honouring what has made us who we are.' He paused, giving them a very meaningful look.

'Maybe some tribe somewhere allows boys your age to participate in hunts,' he said as he began walking around them in slow circles. 'Yes, maybe there are some tribes who do so.'

He seemed thoughtful for a moment, and then whirled around suddenly to point squarely at them. 'But we the Sumi are not that tribe, and we will never be that tribe!

'When we pour our rice beer for the spirits, it isn't to the spirits of other people that we pour, but to the spirits who have been with us since the days of our forefathers. Now, a day may come when you may choose to belong to any tribe you wish, but that day isn't today,' he said with finality. 'Never forget that it is in the tribe that you have your identity and your very safety.'

He exhaled deeply. 'Now whose idea was it then?'

Kato looked down. He was the instigator; there were no two ways about it. He was the one who'd gotten both of them into trouble, dragging his terrified friend into this mess. *Almost gotten them both killed*. He swallowed hard and tasted bitter bile on his tongue. He knew that he ought to take responsibility. It was his to own. He fought back the urge to gag.

'*...he grunts like a beast*,' he heard his aunt's voice in his head over and over again. *Take responsibility!* He felt as though he were falling into himself, a small pathetic lump of a boy. *I am Kato the brave and courageous*. He told himself that he would face the leopard again, risk being torn apart. But this?

'It was my idea, sir,' Apu said. Kato could feel him shaking beside him.

'It was my idea,' Apu repeated, this time in a firmer voice. 'Kato refused but I made him come with me.'

As if in a dream, Kato turned his head and looked at his friend. He noticed for the first time that Apu had a bruise on a cheekbone and dried blood, which looked like a birthmark. He couldn't recognize the boy he was looking at. Apu had always been the timid one, the one who'd pull him back when he wanted to move forward. But this boy by his side had none of the indecision, no pale face or quivering lips. His face instead seemed to shine in the firelight, becoming something intimidating and distant. As though he belonged to light.

'The instigator will get extra lashes,' the chief said in a foreboding voice.

'Please…' Apu pleaded, becoming the boy he knew once more, the boy who would wheedle and plead to get out of trouble. Kato could tell that not all of it was acting because he hadn't stopped shivering. 'We won't do it again. Please!'

The chief glowered. 'There's no question of letting you off. You're not little children anymore.'

'It was I. Let me get the lashes then,' Apu said, the slightest tremor audible in his voice.

Kato knew that he should protest, he knew his friend was just trying to protect him, yet he didn't shake his head, or stand and grunt, or stop his friend from speaking. He just withdrew deeper into himself, feeling small and insignificant as he heard his friend plead for him, imploring the chief that he alone should be punished.

'No, *Imuna awoba qhazu keke, nighi qhazu.* My brother lay down on pig manure and so shall I—that is foolishness. You are no longer suckling children, and you must realize that actions have consequences.

'Kato!' the chief commanded, 'look at me.' Kato lifted his head and met the chief's eyes. 'It was Apu then?' He felt his breath catch in his throat, halfway to courage, yet drowning in despair. *I am Kato the brave and courageous.* Slowly he lowered his eyes to the ground and wished that it would swallow him whole.

'Ten lashes for Apu for instigating things, and five for Kato for following behind blindly. Bring them outside.' The chief pronounced his verdict and went out.

Apu winked at him as he was led to the centre of the circle. The evening was surrendering to dusk and Kato noticed that mercifully none of the children had come to watch. They'd forgotten about him and Apu in the excitement of the merrymaking. Kato watched with a strange sense of detachment as his friend was given the ten lashes on his buttocks and the back of his thighs and calves. He cried and shouted as each lash fell, arching his body like a sun-dried piece of hide and making little hops. He was obviously exaggerating things, for it was obvious that the chief was taking it easy.

He watched Apu walking over to his father after the last lash fell. He tried to find the same distant look on his friend's face once more but there was just the scrawny boy he knew now.

'Kato, come,' the chief commanded. He gestured with the thin branch at the spot where Apu had just been performing his theatrics.

When the first lash landed, he was a whole world away, a world within himself. His father stood among the men, and he imagined the shame he must be feeling watching his mute son being lashed. *Like an animal.* Apu, who'd just taken the lashes meant for him… was he looking at him with accusing eyes? Did he think him a coward? When he felt the hot tears pooling in his eyes it was too late to blink them back; they were already falling to the ground. He wished the lashes would go on longer so that his tears would dry but they ended too soon.

The event ended without any ceremony. No last speech by the chief, no instructions about who was to go or stay. They'd been punished and that was it. With a very abrupt, 'Ahoshe, when is your wife due?' the chief dismissed them.

Kato stood frozen. He'd been the object of so many eyes just a while ago, the subject of so many unknown thoughts. Now even though they'd been dismissed he was unable to extract himself from that position, like a fly that finds itself unexpectedly alone in a spider's web. As his panic began to rise, he felt his father's soft touch on his shoulder. Feeling thankful he let himself be led away from the place. He thought he heard Apu call him, but he didn't look back.

His mother began walking quickly as soon as she saw them. They were still a few houses away from their home, right below the steep path that climbed to Narto's house. Most of the villagers were inside, gathered around hearths, repeating their stories of the day again and again. She quickly took him from his father and pulled him tight. Kato's feet finally found the ground. They walked together the rest of the way, his mother and father on either side, as they'd always been from the start. *Carrying their shame home*. He felt so utterly exhausted.

'Why do you have to make things more difficult for yourself than they already are, my son?' His mother's voice broke. She was finally able to see the extent of the bruises in the lamplight, the big angry welts, the cuts and nicks. Gripping the cloth she'd brought to clean him, she lowered her head on his back and sobbed warm tears on his skin. He simply buried his face in the pillow and counted his heartbeat.

That night, in between feverish sleep and restless waking, Kato dreamt that Apu was as tall as Kene, and he ran furtively, trying to hide from his frail, little friend, who was now a giant.

11

The Tail End of a Betrayal

Kato's mother tapped the ladle on her palm and lapped the rich broth like a cat. Smacking her lips together nosily, she thought briefly before reaching for the salt pot once more. After adding a pinch she stirred the pot and repeated the steps: tap ladle on palm, lick, and a smack of her lips. This time she smiled and nodded to herself. The smell of Kato's favourite dish, smoked pork in axone, filled the kitchen.

He watched from the bench, eyes on his mother, mind on something else. Reaching back, he massaged his bottom with a grimace. It had been two days, but the lashes still ached with a pulsing heat. He'd skipped school the previous day because of two reasons: one, the shame of having to face the class after what had happened, and two, the sudden embarrassment he felt about facing Apu. His friend came by yesterday, but he'd heard and slipped away through the window.

Apu... he sighed. As a child he'd never left his mother's side but he'd noticed the undersized boy who stared at him whenever their mothers met. Kato had taken much longer than other children to understand how words worked and relied on his eyes instead to read people's faces. He did not detect either pity or disgust in Apu's face. He smiled when he remembered the first time they'd met alone. He'd been playing by himself in their courtyard one of the rare times he left his mother's side when a boy's head poked out from behind a tree. It disappeared after a while, only to reappear again behind another tree. Intrigued, Kato followed along and tried to guess where the head would appear next. Without any introductions they played their first game of hide and seek. They'd both been four years old and had been friends since.

And now, he'd betrayed him. He wasn't scared of any lashes, but the thought of the embarrassment on his father's face, and the disgust on the faces of the others had terrified him into silence. There had been no other way. Yet the feeling of shame refused to go away.

He'd never felt any judgment or pity from Apu. He'd never felt lesser than his friend. Apu was the thin boy who was easily scared, and he was the brave boy who couldn't speak. They'd been just fine the way they were. But after what he'd done last night could even Apu stay unchanged? He shook his head furiously and growled. Something had to be done about this.

His mother's face lit up when she saw him hurrying out of the door with his satchel. 'Feeling better, my love?' Kato gave her an embarrassed look and rushed towards Apu's house.

'Have a care, boy!' Lukhashe the toothless old neighbour hailed in his croaky voice. The man took particular delight in scolding children and considering the fact that Kato had been in 'real' trouble just two days prior, he sped up, in no mood for a disapproving sermon.

'Leave the boy alone…' he heard his daughter Hoili tell him.

Kato found Apu's mother weaving on her loom outside. 'Kato, how are you? The lashes still burn?' she asked and began laughing uproariously at the peevish look on his face. Wiping the tears from her eyes, she said in between huge breaths, 'Have a care, you hear, that friend of yours might have dung for brains but you ought to know better. Go in, he's in his room groaning like an *asuyi*.'

Hau, Apu's shaggy, big black dog came to lick him, and followed him into the house barking merrily. He was not a hunting dog and quite useless at just about everything, but he was a merry creature and that was fine for Apu's family. Kato scratched his head fondly as he walked.

'Oh Hau! Fool dog!' Apu shouted from inside. 'Stop barking as if you know everything.' After a pause, he groaned, 'Ah, my poor, frail body. I'm going to die, mother!' Another bout of laughter began outside.

Kato stood for a moment outside Apu's room, not knowing exactly how to approach his friend.

'Come in, you lumbering fool, or I'll tell everyone what a bad child you are,' Apu said, putting on his best old-man voice. Kato went in with a sheepish grin, only to find the imp propped up upon mounds and mounds of shawls and mattresses, smiling wickedly. The sight was so funny that Kato burst out laughing.

Whit, whit, whit... there was a relaxing quality to the sound that made Kato feel meditative. They were inside one of their secret hideouts, under swathes of brush. Between these brushes that grew in huge clumps, two enterprising boys could fashion a sort of pathway leading to a hollow space inside. If done properly, from the outside all people would see were brush, but inside two boys could plot devious things in relative comfort.

Even if Kato had been able to talk, he wouldn't know how to say what he felt. He was lying down on the leaf-strewn ground of the hideout, watching Apu whittle at a stick with his folding knife in the one spot where a bare patch allowed a small circlet of sunshine in. How was he to tell him that ever since he'd let him take responsibility for his deed he'd started harbouring a deep shame. Despite Apu not seeming to care about it one bit, there was no denying the truth, the truth his inner voice gave names—*traitor, coward*... Was his friend just pretending? Did he really not care that he'd had to take the extra lashes meant for him?

I was just about to... I didn't ask him to... As much as he'd tried to find some way to redeem himself there was no escaping the *silence*, his silence. He'd been asked and he'd chosen to look away. He looked at Apu again and recalled the way he'd looked that evening; he'd looked nothing like this funny-looking boy who had a penchant for theatrics. There'd been something unreachable and distant about him then, as if he was looking at the sun from a cold place. *I am a weak coward.* The thought had taken root that evening and it refused to leave.

'Say, ishou,' Apu said, still making thin shavings from the stick, 'what do you think has been going on with the leopard's carcass?'

Now that Apu mentioned it, Kato too wondered. With a quick, wordless glance, it was decided: they would go to the leopard. Apu dutifully folded the little knife and handed it to Kato. He was about to take it but stopped suddenly, a thoughtful look on his face. When the knife was pressed back into Apu's hands his eyes flew wide open, and his mouth turned into a big, wide O.

'I can't, ishou,' he protested a little half-heartedly, 'I know how much you love this knife.'

Kato kept pressing it into his hands desperately.

'Aizao! What a grand present, Ishou!' Apu couldn't stop saying, as he folded and unfolded the little knife on their way towards the village gate. He was right, Kato had treasured the thing since he'd found it three years ago. Kato knew that Apu liked it a great deal too, and seeing the joy on his friend's face made his guilt recede just a little. However, a part of him knew—he'd chosen silence once more. Kato hastily crawled his way out as if he were running away from something.

The boys could see the carcass of the leopard from far away. It was strapped to the bamboo platform, and even from where they were the stench of the rotting animal was offensive.

'Mmmppfff! Idou lesh gnn bak,' Apu said with his nose between two fingers. Kato had to agree because the stench was truly terrible, but just as he was about to turn away, he remembered the befuddlement on the leopard's face. He motioned his friend to wait for him there while he went closer. Apu being Apu followed anyway, gagging and snorting.

If the stench had been unbearable before, by the time they reached the carcass it was positively deadly. Kato had to fight very hard to stop his stomach from heaving all its contents out, and from Apu's pinched nose and bright red face he wasn't faring any better.

Through teary eyes Kato saw that the leopard's skin was starting to mottle, and through the spear wounds maggots could be seen crawling inside. The flies, fat and shiny, did their work with the most meticulous precision—flitting here and there—all the while making the most awful droning buzzing. The fur of the animal had small bumps that moved when the maggots underneath entered one of their feeding frenzies.

It was almost too much to bear even for Kato, and his friend evidently had had enough. One hand gripping Kato's arm, he desperately tried to steer him away from the foul place. But Kato wasn't leaving before seeing what he had come to see.

He swatted at the flies that covered the leopard's head in a mass of black wings, bodies and frenetic feet. They roared away angrily to reveal the leopard's eyes—big empty sockets filled with squirming white things. Kato finally had enough, and together the boys ran away, retching and vomiting all over themselves.

With bitter mouths and emptied stomachs, they washed themselves at the spring, praying that neither of their mothers would choose this most untimely moment to come fetch water.

'Boy! You are one crazy fellow!' Apu swore angrily. 'Upon my mother's name! I nearly passed out!' Kato closed his eyes, feeling the cool air beginning to dry his wet skin. His friend had every right to be angry; after all he had cost them their lunches. But it had needed to be done.

A snarling, potent creature of fury had been reduced to a macabre feast for maggots, flies, and winged scavengers, no more able to answer his question now than when it had been alive— *what stopped your mad rage from tearing us apart?*

Kene would know.

He saw his grandmother sitting outside with his mother when he got home.

'Little squirrel, just the person I came to see!' his grandmother said happily when she saw him. 'You smell!' his mother said when he came closer. 'Go get changed, your apuza wants you to take her somewhere.' His grandmother fondly tussled his hair, not minding the stench of vomit. He smiled at her and went in to change.

'He's growing into a fine young man, Nisheli,' he heard his grandmother say from outside.

'Oh mother, please talk some sense into that thick head of his or he'll get into worse trouble next time.'

His grandmother laughed light-heartedly. 'He's a young boy, let him have his occasional mistakes.'

'Little squirrel, you did wrong by disobeying the law of the village,' his grandmother said as they walked towards the eastern side of the village. She grinned, seeing his shocked expression. 'Overheard me talking with your mother, did you?' She always seemed to know what he was thinking. The rooster in his right hand shifted nervously and cackled.

'Yes, little boys need to be allowed your mistakes without too much scolding, but what you and Apu did was very stupid. The law of our people exists for our own good. Imagine what would happen if other children too decided that it was okay for them to sneak to the hunt. There would be parents crying over their dead children all over the village today instead of just two boys with fiery buttocks.' Kato gave her a sheepish look, knowing full well that she spoke the truth.

'Maybe you boys were just lucky, or maybe it was something else, but you saw the leopard. Would it have been worth the risk if it had gotten to you with its claws and fangs?'

Kato shook his head woefully. They walked on in silence for a while.

'How scared were you, little squirrel?' his grandmother whispered conspiratorially, a smile lurking on her mouth. Kato knocked his knees together and shivered with a terror-stricken look, which drew forth a full laugh out of her and a terrified cackle out of the rooster. 'Let this be the last of it!' she said with iron in her voice, and inwardly Kato agreed with her most whole-heartedly.

To his great distress, his grandmother kept walking past the village boundary, towards the lone hut that lay on the damp side of the mountain. Kato grabbed her hand with his free one, not quite willing to let his fear show, but undeniably terrified. 'She's harmless, Kato, and more importantly, she's my friend. No need to be afraid.' He quickly pulled his hand back, quite offended at being accused of being afraid.

Ghonili's hut was a small thing that looked far older than any other house in the village. There was a trickle of smoke that drifted up lazily through one side of the bamboo house. Nothing else suggested that anyone lived there.

'Ipami! My friend!' his grandmother hailed to no one in particular as they closed in on the hut.

Ghonili came out of the hut so promptly that he wondered whether she had been expecting them. A shiver went through him. '...*Flies with the devils, cooks babies alive, digs people's graves, sends spirits to do her bidding...*' Without knowing how it got there he found his hand clutching the edge of his grandmother's shawl, mercifully not as emasculating as grabbing her hand again.

'Ipami, it's been a while,' Ghonili said quite normally, much to Kato's amazement. His grandmother must be quite a great woman for even the witch to speak to her so. Kato warily followed his grandmother into the hut behind Ghonili.

The hut consisted of a single room with a smallish hearth in the middle and a small platform towards a lone window. Bedclothes and shawls were stacked against the thatch wall in neat bundles. 'The breeze is nice here,' Ghonili said, gesturing towards the open window. She didn't take the lead herself but waited. His grandmother smiled at the witch and walked to the platform. Kato quickly sat down beside his grandmother on the wooden floor. He heaved a sigh of relief when Ghonili sat down by the hearth instead of joining them.

'How have you been, ipami?'

'Not too poorly I suppose,' Ghonili replied with a fond grin.

Kato peered around as the two women talked. It wasn't as he'd expected at all. As old as it looked and as small as it was, he had to admit that for one lone person it would do very well. A few pots and dishes glimmered by the hearth. No cobwebs or spiders hung from the ceiling. It was really a very clean house.

A wave of relief swept over him, and a little disappointment too. There was nothing very scary about the old woman. No terrible things hanging inside her hut, no shadows following her, no rotting babies' corpses, no eerie sounds, just a lonely old woman who seemed very glad to have an old friend visit her. He absently looked down from the ceiling and saw her looking at him. There was a mocking smile lurking on her lips, as though she were making fun of him for believing all the stuff the other children said about her. He wriggled his toes and slid closer to his grandmother.

'This one has a smell about him,' she told his grandmother, gesturing at him with her chin. Kato felt very uncomfortable.

'Hmmm…' His grandmother peered closely at him, looking like a curious swan.

She knows about Kene! Kato panicked. *But how!*

'Nothing to worry, just something…' Ghonili trailed away absently. Kato heaved in relief, watching his grandmother out the corner of an eye. She didn't seem to have caught on. His eyes swung to the tu-umi and found her regarding him with a stern look.

'Leopards are not naughty boys.'

Kato understood what she meant to say and could do nothing except look away.

'Hush! Old friend, you have given me much more than I can ever repay you for,' his grandmother said as they stood outside the door.

'Kato, do you know that when you were a very small boy you became very ill, and it was your grandma Ghonili who cured you with her leaves!' Kato gaped like an idiot and couldn't think of anything to do, except look down at his feet. The witch cackled with mirth.

'Ghonili saw spirits and things other people cannot from a very young age—a shixi, people with the second sight,' Kato's grandmother began on their way home.

'Her first husband married her when she was just thirteen. They had no children, and he died within two years of their marriage. She became a young widow at fifteen, but her skills with medicinal leaves and roots that she had learned from her mother kept her fed and clothed since the villagers gave her things for curing them of their ailments. Both her parents died not long after, and being the only child, talk of her being unlucky started.

'She still lived in the village then, and a young man became besotted with her. Against the advice of his relatives, he married her. There used to be a glow to her those days, a cheerful joy that soon had people rethinking their judgement.' His grandmother shook her head with pleasure, remembering the happiness of her friend. 'Such a beauty she was!'

'However, her joy was not long-lived. Two years after this second marriage her husband became very sick, and despite all her skills, he died soon after, leaving her a childless widow for the second time. The trickling talks of her being unlucky now became a torrent. No one asked her to leave but I suppose staying in the village became unbearable for her. She left and started living where she lives now. People still went to her for her cures, but to them she became something like one of her bitter medicines, useful but not favoured.'

Kato thought the whole thing unfair, and it occurred to him that they were not dissimilar. Both misunderstood, preferring to be ignored. 'That is why you should never be unkind to people, my little squirrel. Who knows what stories they have…' she trailed off melancholically.

'I know many do not approve of my friendship with her, but she was my friend once and she still is.' Kato glanced at her and felt himself blush when he remembered what he'd done to his own friend just a few days ago. They walked back in silence the rest of the way.

12

A Storyteller?

It was finally here. The moon, an unbroken circle, hung pendulously outside. Kato lifted a tentative finger and teased the gossamer strand of almost-light that flitted in through the thatch. Last night had been a complete waste; despite the moon's roundness Kene hadn't shown up and he'd gone to sleep disappointed.

This time, mixed in with the anticipation, there was a cloying sense of dread. *He cannot know,* he thought to himself for the hundredth time. He remembered Kene's words from their last meeting: *'If only you knew how difficult it is to speak the truth you wouldn't think it so easy.'* He imagined different scenarios in his mind if Kene were to find out about what had happened; all of them ended with the giant pronouncing him unfit for the task. *He cannot know.* It would all end: the stories, the adventures, the speaking... Kene's promise. Kato caught the moonlight on his palm and shivered inside.

Why does he always have to do this? He'd been waiting a long time, and his body was becoming very uncooperative.

He willed his tired eyes to stay open, but finally it became too hard to stay awake and he fell asleep, the rapidly receding conscious part of his mind worrying that he might not hear if Kene called.

He must not know.

'Kato, Kato, wake up, little friend.'

In an instant he was awake but this time he didn't rush outside as he usually did.

'Kato, Kato,' Kene called again. A part of him wondered how much longer the giant would wait if he didn't answer. Perhaps he'd leave after the next call. Perhaps he'd leave if he didn't answer this time. *Perhaps he wouldn't return. Perhaps that would be best.* His heart beat like a drum. Finally unable to fight the suspense anymore he slowly walked outside, but first he dug out his grandmother's gift and spread it on his back. The warmth comforted him. He found Kene on one knee under the bright moonlight. 'You came,' Kato said with his most neutral expression. 'Hahaha…' The deep rumble of Kene's laugh made his mouth curve up despite his mood. It sounded just the way he remembered it, like boulders rolling down a mountainside.

Without a word he ran and clambered first onto Kene's knee, and then up to his shoulder, bringing forth another delighted rumble. 'How has my little storyteller been?' Kene asked.

'Let's go!' Kato replied, regretting the gruffness of his reply already. *Tonight isn't going to be easy.*

Something struck Kato as they went their way. 'Tell me, Kene, why do you only come when I am asleep?' A gurgling sound reverberated out of the giant's belly. Kato realized that it was mirthful guffawing.

'It is a game that I play with you, little friend,' he said.

'What game?'

'It is my game, and only I know the rules, so hush!'

Kato knew enough not to ask further though irritation poked its prickly head in his mind.

They passed a family of sloth bears rooting among some roots. Noticing young cubs amongst them Kato shrunk back, making himself small; Kato knew well enough about mother bears and their aggression. Thankfully, they paid them no mind and continued their business. *Probably because I'm with Kene,* Kato thought with relief. Except for the nocturnal kinds they hardly ever came across animals out and about.

Kato was shocked when after a good deal of walking Kene deposited him on the same grassy clearing beyond which stood the giant Lakhe. They'd taken the path south of the village tonight while usually on other nights they'd gone west. *Another one of his secrets no doubt,* he thought, not bothering to ask anymore.

Kato squiggled his feet on the soft grass and looked around. The big boulder still sat under the one patch of clear sky from which the moon's silvery light shone, bathing it in gentle luminescence. He walked up to it and began tracing patterns on its dimpled surface.

'Here, drink this,' Kene said from behind him. Kato hadn't noticed him approaching. Turning around he took the proffered leaf-cup wordlessly and drank deep. His anxious mind only absently noticed the freshness of the water. Once he was done, he walked away from the boulder and pretended to study the vegetation. He felt a tightness in his chest, dreading what might come next.

'Come here, Kato,' Kene called to him from the boulder.

He slowly ambled his way to the giant, dragging his feet across the soft grass.

'Is something the matter?' Kene asked with a concerned look. Kato shook his head and went back to tracing patterns on the boulder. *He's going to find out!* his inner voice screamed. Tiny beads of sweat began to collect around his hairline and above his lips. He'd never been good at deception.

'Okay, that's good,' Kene said. 'Shall we go up then?'

His insides rolled into a tight ball as Kene swiftly had him lashed to his body once more. As soon as their climb began, one mighty heave at a time, Kato began to keep count to distract his mind from both the fear of the height as well as the anxiety that had come to possess his mind. *One, two...*

No matter how many times they did this, climbing Lakhe would always be nerve-wracking. 'Not to worry, not to worry...' Kene kept repeating as he climbed higher and higher, never missing a step or fumbling for a hold. *One hundred eighty-six,* Kato counted, and they finally ran out of trunk and there was simply the openness.

'So then, Kato my friend,' the giant rumbled, quite comfortably settled on the platform. 'What have you been up to since the last time we met?'

Kato froze like a mesmerized rooster. *Does he know?* He could feel his pulse wreaking havoc inside his chest. It felt as though he would go deaf from the pounding in his ears. He put in every ounce of determination to keep his voice from giving away his secret.

'What do you mean?'

'Well, tell me the interesting bits, little friend.'

He doesn't know. Relief swept over him, and in equal measure the pressure of having to keep up the façade. *How much should I say?* Everything would end. *Tell him only what he needs to know,* the inner voice said.

'There was a hunt, a leopard hunt,' he began haltingly.

Kene immediately became attentive. 'A leopard hunt, you say?'

Kato looked at him closely, studying his expression. What he saw there would decide which way his story would go.

'Hmmm...' Kene sighed. He looked sad.

I should tell him the truth. Every breath had begun to hurt, and his chest felt like it was turning to stone. He imagined the disappointed look on Kene's face.

'It was injured and had become a danger to the villagers.' *He must not know. It will end.* A trickle of sweat dripped onto his lips, and he quickly wiped it away.

'Ah, so it was,' Kene said, looking oddly like a thoughtful rooster. 'So it was…'

Kato swallowed before continuing. 'Apu and I went to watch the hunt.'

Kene narrowed his eyes. 'Is that allowed for boys your age?'

'No, we disobeyed the village rules.'

'Hmmm…' *What did that mean?*

'Hmmm…' *Pay closer attention!*

His head ached with the strain he was putting on it. 'Things went wrong…'

'Huh?' Kene straightened his back and sat up with a sudden movement.

'The leopard found us in our hiding place…'

Kene stood up alarmed, exclaiming something in a strange tongue. Kato flinched as if he'd been struck. *Does he know?* He waited for Kene to turn around and looked at his face. *Concern.*

'It was mad with pain… enraged.' He remembered the snarling, terror-maddened visage of the enraged beast and shivered. *What stopped your mad rage from tearing us apart?*

Kene waited for him to continue, looking like a breathless young boy.

'It just stood there, it just stood there…' Kato blinked in renewed disbelief. It still felt like an impossible dream.

'That's all?' Kene asked.

Kato thought for a moment. 'It smelled me… it smelled me and just stood there.'

'Hmmm...' With a satisfied expression on his face Kene nodded seriously. 'Smelled *me* on you it did. Smelled an *old one* on a human child.'

Kato sat with his mouth open. *Of course! Animals have much better noses than men. Kene had saved him.*

'Go on then,' Kene asked.

Careful now! Kato's mind made an impossible number of calculations, desperately seeking a way out of this mess he was in. 'My father speared it, and it died in front of me...' He felt panic rising inside. The memory of pink blood made his hair stand on ends and a chill ran through him. He didn't understand the need to be so detailed, but he continued as though something else had a hold on him. *Careful now!* 'It died... And I am safe.' He felt as if he were in a stupor.

'That's the way it is sometimes,' Kene said with a bittersweet smile. 'Go on.'

'They caught us and took us to be punished.' Kato chose his next words very carefully, as though they would decide the entirety of what was to follow in his life. 'Ten lashes *each* for Apu and I.

'Ten lashes each,' he repeated, making himself believe. *Willed* himself to believe. The breath he'd been holding inside became fire that charred his lungs. Clenching his teeth, he looked away, terrified that his eyes would give it all away.

'Small price to pay for such great foolishness,' Kene pronounced solemnly.

Kato exhaled gratefully. *He does not suspect anything!* He reminded himself that the only other option would have ended this part of his life forever. *No harm done. No harm done. No harm done.* His galloping heart began to settle into a rhythm that wasn't trying to rip his chest apart.

He'd successfully hidden his betrayal from Kene. That should have been the end of it. There was no disbelief in Kene's face. It was a very small lie anyway. Yet a different kind of misery began to take root. While the fear had felt like fire in his lungs, this new misery felt like a rock wedged in his throat.

'You boys were reckless,' Kene rumbled disapprovingly. Kato's mind screeched to a stop.

Kene sighed, leaned back against the trunk, and looked at Lakhe's branches. 'So young still,' he said to himself.

Kato took great care in rearranging his legs, making sure not to make eye contact with Kene.

'It might seem the same to you, Kato, but there is a great difference between recklessness and courage.'

Kato's defences went up the moment he heard the word 'courage'. *Does he know that I am a coward?* Perhaps he did. He waited, now attentively considering Lakhe's bark.

'Look here, my little friend,' Kene commanded. Kato gritted his teeth and lifted his eyes.

'Recklessness is selfish and purposeless,' Kene explained. 'What would your deaths have achieved if things had gone wrong?' He waited for an answer, looking at Kato intently.

Kene was right. Kato imagined what their parents would have gone through if instead of a few lashes they'd brought home dead sons. His grandmother had told him the same thing. He shook his head.

'That's right,' Kene said, softening his voice. 'You'd have caused so much pain.'

'Now courage,' he continued, soft but firm. 'Courage isn't thoughtless. It is considerate and sacrificing. That is what you must have to become a storyteller.'

Kato felt his eyes begin to waver and lowered them once more. He'd put himself through agony to deceive Kene, and succeeded. Yet, the outcome was the same—he was being told that he was not good enough to be a storyteller. Granted, not

in those terms, but still… *That is what you must have to become a storyteller.* He knew that given the same situation he'd choose silence again.

'Is it possible to never be afraid?' he found himself asking.

'Courage, my friend, couldn't exist without fear,' Kene answered kindly, emphasizing each word. 'Yes, there are some who'd disagree with me, though how different such courage is from madness I couldn't tell.' He shook his head with a distant smile. 'But the best kind! The best kind exists *despite* the fear.'

Kato closed his eyes and went back to that evening in the council hall. He recalled Apu's shivering and that strange look a few heartbeats later. *He should have chosen Apu instead*, he found himself thinking bitterly.

'A storyteller must be courageous above all things because truth requires courage,' Kene continued. 'The truth is often not agreeable to people. Sometimes you will even have to tell stories that you do not like. You will need courage then, because if you let yourself be carried along by fear the stories will no longer matter.'

Kato felt like a complete phony. He wanted to be the boy his apuza and Kene wanted him to be—a boy who'd always tell the truth, a courageous boy. *Someone like Apu?* The thought drove a stake inside his guts. But none of them knew what it was to not have a voice. None of them were *him*!

'I did not ask to be a storyteller!' the words came out bitter. Kene lifted a shaggy eyebrow and simply stared at him.

'I'm sorry, I did not mean it like that,' Kato said apologetically after a while.

'Hmmm… I understand,' Kene said. 'There *is* so much for you to learn, but there's just not enough time. Change is almost here.'

They sat wordlessly for a while.

'Why don't you tell me about that beautiful shawl you have?' Kene asked.

Kato untied it from his body and passed it to him. 'My grandmother wove it for me,' he said.

It looked tiny in Kene's hands. He ran his hand over it with a smile. 'I'd like to have a grandmother too,' he said. 'Does it mean anything?'

Kato didn't reply immediately, looking instead at the moon that was dipping in the sky lazily. 'No, it's just a shawl. It means nothing.'

13

Two Tales by Flowing Waters

Tok, Tok, Tok! 'Sit still, Kato,' his father commanded. *Tok, Tok, Tok.* He felt the cold metal of the dao against his skin shift to another position behind his ears. He trusted his father implicitly but today the sound of the razor-sharp edge brushing up against his hair sent little needles down his spine. He was getting a haircut the traditional Sumi way. Lining up the edge of the dao under a bunch of hair, his father began striking it with a stick again. *Tok, Tok, Tok.* The traditional haircut was a very severe crop that began high above the forehead, continued well above the ears on both sides and completed a disc high at the back. His hair grew very fast and so this was a ritual he and his father performed every month. The loose hair fell on his shoulder like a ghost's caress.

'How handsome you are, ilomi!' his mother exclaimed, clapping her hands, as she walked up to them. He rolled his eyes. He hadn't been in a good mood lately. His face settled into a glum look as he recalled the nightmare from last night. They'd become more frequent, the bad dreams. Since his betrayal of Apu and the subsequent meeting with Kene, his happiness seemed to be leaking away, bit by bit. 'We go to set fish traps tomorrow, son.' His father's voice jolted him from his daydream. He blew strands of hair from his skin when the haircut was deemed satisfactory.

He nodded absently. He could see his parents exchange a look. He knew what they were up to. Usually the prospect of a fishing trip with his father would have him whopping in delight.

'You'll have so much fun!' his mother said. He gave her a wan smile and went to take a bath.

⸺

The greyness of the early hour complemented the sombre cantata of the crickets. Kato waited as his father strapped two bamboo river traps onto his shoulder and slung the remaining three on his own back. It was late summer, but in the mountains, it was always cold in the mornings, and it would be especially so down by the river. He pulled the ends of his worn old shawl closer. His grandmother's beautiful, ebony one was folded away and tucked in neatly amongst his belongings. He couldn't bear to look at it now.

'Don't be too late,' his mother called to them from the kitchen where she was bent over the hearth, coaxing smoky embers to life. He heard her hacking cough. Some rain had leaked into the woodpile and the wood was being very uncooperative. It was as though all the smoke in the world had come to occupy the kitchen they'd just left behind moments before.

The neighbour's dog came barking as they passed by, and went back sniffing in disgust at being roused from his sleep by their unremarkable selves. Kato blew warm air into his cupped hands and rubbed them together furiously, trying to warm them up in anticipation of the cold work that awaited him and his father. He hurried to catch up with his father who had left him behind. He was a very tall man and keeping up with him was always a task for his mother and him. His father had his own pace and often carried on, unaware of how far ahead or behind he was. It was the same way with how he did everything else in life. Unexpectedly, today he stopped and turned around to wait for him to catch up. 'The fish will still be sleeping,' his father said, 'we lay the traps in the night or before dawn or else they will avoid the traps.' Kato already knew this but he nodded.

Wordlessly they came down to the river where mist hung over the flowing currents like a stubborn afterthought. They had come to lay traps many times before, and by now they had their own preferred nooks and crannies that they alternated between. Coming to one such place, Lhokashe unslung a trap and handed it to Kato. 'Show me,' he said.

Kato took it and straddled two rocks between which he wedged the bamboo trap. The fish would swim into the trap through the mouth, and get trapped because of a clever contraption that allowed entry, while prohibiting escape. If they were lucky, when they returned in the evening there would be fishes the size of thumbs, and if they were extremely lucky, perhaps there would also be aghungu, a kind of mountain trout that tasted uncommonly good. Taking a goodly sized rock Kato placed it on top of the trap's wedge-shaped behind to secure it against the strong currents. His father nodded in approval, and they continued onwards.

After the second trap was placed, his father began as usual in his abrupt fashion, 'Do you know about rivers, my son?'

Kato looked at his father in befuddlement. What was there to know about rivers? They were mighty sometimes and trickled some other times, but they flowed just the same.

'You might think that rivers are just flowing water, but they have a will just like you and me. Listen well, my son, and I will tell you about rivers.'

'It is about a time long ago. On a mountain, beside the mighty river Wozu, stood the village called Wozu-phu, so called for the sake of the river. It was not a very big village, and its people were prosperous for the river gave life to the soil. All was good with them, but like a storm come unawares a great dispute began over a much-treasured damsel. The girl, who belonged to a great clan, refused all suitors from other big clans in the village because she had fallen in love with a boy from a small clan. Despite all attempts to dissuade her she refused to be swayed, and so the girl's clan went and threatened the boy, but he too refused to budge.

'Enraged by this defiance the girl's clan planned a wicked scheme, and when the whole village slept one night they went armed with daos and spears to kill the boy, but they couldn't find him at home. You see, the girl had come to know of the scheme and had run away with her lover, but sadly she had come to know of it very late. Her enraged family pursued them and caught them by the river where they caught hold of the boy, murdered him and threw his body into the raging currents. Maddened by the death of her love the damsel tore free of her captors, and threw herself into the churning water after his body, crying "O ilomi! O ilomi!" She was carried away then, and her body was never found.

'It is said that the river which bore witness to this great injustice could not abide there anymore, and over a single night changed its course to flow in a different direction, away from the village. Slowly the land surrounding the village wasted away for the river had carried its life away with it, and soon the cursed village stood in ruins, abandoned and deserted.

'So you see,' his father continued, 'rivers are alive and they have a will.'

Kato felt a great sadness for the two lovers who'd been so unjustly dealt with. Silently, they walked on as the river gurgled and roared, and Kato began to feel like there were words being repeated again and again amongst the roaring. 'Osihe! Oishe! Oishe! How sad! How sad!' It made the hairs on the back of his neck stand and he wondered if perhaps, rivers told each other stories too. He made a mental note to ask Kene about rivers and their will when they met next.

When they reached home the kitchen no longer looked like the haunt of some smoke monster. His mother cheerily handed them hot steaming cups of corn soup and to his surprise Kato found that despite his misgivings his mood had lifted a little.

'To the river! To the river! Where little fish wait, little fish with white bellies, to tickle our hungry bellies!' Apu chanted and danced. Kato hurried and tried to keep up, wondering just what it was that had his friend in such high spirits. He blanched when the obvious answer occurred to him. Narto!

His father had gone to attend a meeting at the council hall and it had fallen to him and his friend to retrieve the fish traps. Apu took out a toy from his satchel. It was a simple one that consisted of a wooden handle, and a small bamboo stem with holes that was strung to the top of the handle with twine. When the handle was swung in the hand it would make the bamboo pipe go round and round, and air would enter the holes making a sound that was like that of a flute. The faster the toy was swung, the louder the sound would get and the higher its pitch went. '*Whoom, whoom, whoom, wheee, whee...*' it went as the two boys made their way down to the river.

'*...whether you are to be a storyteller or not we shall see when we get to it.*' Was there really any point in continuing his adventures with Kene? He looked at his friend ahead of him and remembered the look on his face from that evening. A cold trickle of despair slid down his throat. *But he came for me!* He fought back. *He must know something.* Hastily shutting down the questions that had begun to froth within him he ran to catch up with Apu.

They were in luck. The first basket didn't have anything in it besides a type of water insect, whose name translated into 'mother of crab', but the second basket was a completely different matter. Kato knew that it was full of fish, for even from afar he could see it shaking as the fish inside tried to escape. There were twelve fish inside, even mountain trout, and one long eel the size of a finger. Apu whooped with delight and Kato gurgled along, which was what his chuckle sounded like.

'I swear, Aghungu cooked with achepho, ginger and green chilli is the best food in the whole, wide world!' Apu declared as he untied the trapdoor and handed the fishes to Kato, who put them into a cane basket lined with green banana leaves. Kato had to agree with his friend for the trout truly tasted divine.

The third had eight fishes in it, five of them aghungu! The fourth was something of a mystery, for it was not at the spot Kato had wedged it in, but on the banks, where it lay like an abandoned toy. There were teeth marks on the tough bamboo, but it was otherwise intact. The trap was still wet so whatever animal had tried to get inside, and Kato thought he knew which animal it was, must have been startled by their approach. This basket was clogged with fishes and even a few river crabs; no wonder the otter had tried to get inside. Today the river was truly in a most generous mood, and Kato thought that perhaps it was showing its appreciation for his father's story by its banks in the morning. He left a middling-sized fish on the sand for his hairy little friend.

'Ishou, do you think about the leopard hunt sometimes?'

Kato fumbled with the hatch of the trap he was handling. His ears suddenly seemed to catch on fire. Busying himself even more with the trap, he pretended to not have heard the question.

'Ishou, did you hear me?' Apu asked, louder this time.

Feeling annoyance rising inside him Kato nodded. He did not want to dwell on the hunt at all.

Apu thwacked him on the back loudly and guffawed. 'I peed myself but thankfully no one noticed in the excitement.'

Kato shrugged dismissively and continued walking to the final trap. *Why is he bringing the hunt up all of a sudden?* He fumed inside.

'Were you scared, Ishou?' Apu asked. He caught up to him and put a thin arm around his shoulder. 'Don't lie now,' he whispered. 'I felt you shivering too when the leopard came for us!' He began guffawing again.

Is he making fun of me? Kato flung his friend's arm off and thundered ahead. The imp wouldn't stop laughing and followed behind like a vengeful ghost.

Just then they came across the discarded skin of a very large snake. It was lying on a sun-bleached rock. Remarkably unbroken, it looked like someone's discarded shawl. *I'll show him!* Kato flung the fish traps off his back and ran to it. When he began to poke at it with a stick Apu made a disgusted sound.

'Eizei! Ishou, will you please stop doing that!' he shouted, looking as if he expected the skin to come to life and slither after them at any moment. Kato goaded his friend with his eyes. *Scared, are you?* The blood fled from Apu's face when he saw the look in Kato's eyes and he tried to pull him away. Taking a deep breath Kato reached for the snakeskin with his bare hand.

'NO!' Apu shouted looking aghast, as he barrelled into him, knocking him onto the hard pebbles. Both of them yelped together in pain.

'You touch that and your skin will become scaly like a snake's, you fool!' Apu shouted. Kato lay back on the pebble-strewn ground, completely at the mercy of the hacking laughter that shook his body. Looking sideways at Apu's pale face he smiled to himself. *I am Kato the brave.* Feeling in much better spirits he stood up and offered a hand to his friend. Apu grumbled and took his hand, and after a while he began to laugh too. 'You're an idiot, you know,' he said, as they continued on.

'Oi, ishou, that snakeskin has reminded me of a story I heard before, when I was young, you know.' Kato rolled his eyes at the last part. Apu had an affectation where he pretended to be some old man, referring to even people his age as 'child' or 'dear son' or 'dear daughter'.

'Anyway, the story... Long ago, when our grandparents weren't even born yet, two men went down to the rivulet one night to catch frogs. This rivulet was not as big as a river, but certainly much bigger than a stream. Now, these two froggers were expecting a great haul, like they had two big baskets you know, but even they were amazed at what they saw there. The rivulet was dry, and there were fish and frogs floundering on its bed going, flip-flop, flip-flop!'

Kato looked at his friend suspiciously, thinking he was spinning another one of his tall tales.

'Oh! Come on now! It's a real story! Ashoqhimushi! I swear!' Apu said, biting on his bent forefinger as an oath. Kato raised his eyebrows, still not convinced completely, but nodded at his friend to continue.

'Okay, so the rivulet was dry. They were naturally amazed and began to follow it up stream to see what the matter was.' He paused for effect here. 'Of course they left the fish and frogs alone,' he added as an afterthought, and Kato nodded in agreement, for taking them given the unnaturalness of the situation would be a forbidden thing—a genna.

'They kept walking until, in the pale moonlight, they saw a huge tree that had fallen across the river blocking its path. The mystery though was where the tree had come from because such a tree had never grown there. They were still puzzling at it when they both stopped in horror, for they saw the tree move! You see, it was no tree but a giant python that was lying across the rivulet, blocking the water and stopping its currents. Gripped by paralyzing fear, it took them a while before they came to their senses, but you better believe that they ran as fast as they could back to the village. Both of them became terribly feverish for their souls had been grievously injured by the fright, and while one of them did recover, the other never woke up from his fever and died.' Apu ended the story ominously.

In the long silence following the story, the sounds of the river echoing from the rocks and trees seemed to become strange and alien to Kato's ears, and he felt the hairs on his arms and the nape of his neck stand up. The setting sun carved out dark nooks and corners everywhere, and every one of them seemed to be hiding something frightening. He remembered his grandmother's story, and all of a sudden their smallness became amplified when contrasted with the seemingly endless expanse that surrounded them, and an urgent need to turn around and run came over him. When he looked at his friend it became obvious from his dry, pale mouth that the storyteller too had fallen into the thrall of his own story, and in a moment of wordless agreement they both yelled and started running back to the village as fast as they could, the last fish trap completely forgotten.

They ran and ran, blood pounding in their ears, their heads swollen and heavy with fright. Only when they were past the village gates did they stop to catch their breaths and consider the damage to the fishes, which had bounced around in the baskets as they ran. Thankfully, though they looked a little rough they were still recognizably fishes, and the two boys heaved a sigh of relief as they laid down on the ground in utter exhaustion.

=

Long after Apu had left with fish that his mother wrapped in banana leaf—his share for helping—Kato sat on his bed, still feeling weak from the running, wondering how he would ever go back to his small retreat by the riverside alone. Of course, the good thing about stories is that though they scare you sometimes it wears away quickly, and we go back to doing what we do.

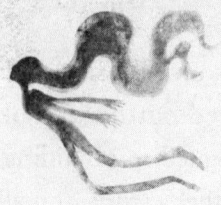

14

Weavings

'Are rivers living, Kene?'

'Hmmm...' Kene rumbled, making the air tremble and Kato's nose twitch. He remembered the first night they'd met when Kene had made his door tremble.

'And how is it that you're asking this, my little friend?' Even though they weren't looking at each other Kato detected a smile playing on Kene's mouth.

'My father told me a story about how rivers are alive and have a will.'

'Tell me the story,' Kene requested.

Kato took his time, recalling as best as he could his father's story. When he came to the part where the young damsel followed her lover into the churning ruin of the torrential river, his heart squeezed inside his chest.

'Ah, yes,' Kene said approvingly. 'There are all sorts of stories as you well know, my friend, but you'll be most pleased to know that your father's story is true as true can be.'

Kato clapped his hands like a happy child. It was so nice to hear someone as special as Kene say such a nice thing about his father. He admired his father's quiet determination, his resilient doggedness, his steady love for both him and his mother. But people seldom pay attention to a quiet man, too busy with the lure of beautiful words and pleasing sounds.

'Rivers *are* alive, as are the mountains, and a storyteller would do well to remember this. For if they are alive it stands to reason that they can be killed too.'

Kato stared at Kene in shock. *Kill rivers and mountains?*

'You disbelieve me? As from very, very far away I've heard with my own ears the final keening of dying mountains and rivers.' Kene's voice became distant. 'Your kind have become far too powerful elsewhere and have laid waste to the land. It is a thing that could make one weep forever.'

Kato shivered and rubbed his arms furiously, choosing to look away. It sounded as though in that moment Kene were blaming him too for what was happening elsewhere, just because he too was human.

Kene's eyes suddenly narrowed. 'We have a visitor.'

Kato's scalp tingled, and he turned around quickly.

'Don't worry.' Kene smiled wryly. 'She's just curious, that's all.'

'Who?' Kato got a very strong sense that someone was approaching him, yet there was no one there. His eyes tracked the feeling instead of what they saw. It would draw near and then retreat, dart here and there, almost like a playful child. It seemed to be observing him . . . like a predator its prey? Kato's heart pounded in his chest.

'She's just curious,' Kene repeated. 'There's no need to worry.'

Is he able to see it? The presence drew all the way back to the edge of the platform. His eyes darted to Kene, and he saw him looking at the same spot his senses pointed at.

'Go on then,' Kene said gently.

He squinted and, from the corner of his eye, saw something in the moonlight that looked like summer mist, almost there, but impossibly so. Then in the blink of an eye it leapt off the platform and was gone!

'Who was that!' Kato jumped to his feet and rubbed his exposed arms furiously.

'Your people call her the muza muza,' Kene said simply.

'The muza muza?' Kato felt his face go numb. He'd grown up hearing so many stories about people who'd disappeared and were later found in the most unlikely places. Wandering inside caves, terrified and witless on treetops and sheer cliff faces, sometimes in faraway places they'd never been before. Muza muza. It was all supposed to be its work. It had been here, with him just a moment ago!

'How do you know it?' He shuddered and scooted closer to Kene.

'*Her*,' Kene corrected. 'You may not believe it, but she was once one of my kind. I stayed with the land, but she strayed. She became lost and now you call her muza muza.'

'Why does she abduct people?' Kato asked.

'That is complicated,' Kene replied. 'It is not so much that she abducts people…' he began slowly. 'There are pathways, Kato, just like the paths in your village. But unlike yours, these pathways you cannot see. The animals have their own pathways they use, your kind has your own pathways, and so do we, the *old ones*. It is the creator that made them so.'

'Go on.'

'When the muza muza strayed, she left our pathways and became trapped in the in-between. Not having her own pathway, she crosses over into other pathways every now and then. It is then that certain people with a weak will follow her out. These you think of as abducted when in reality they followed her…'

'Is such a thing possible? These pathways you speak of?' It sounded utterly far-fetched, but Kene was serious as serious can be.

'How do you think were-tigers came to be?'

'Men who crossed over into the pathways of tigers?'

Kene nodded.

As unbelievable as it sounded, it made sense. Old Futhena was a confirmed were-tiger and though his tiger form too was known to have aged with its human owner, any spotting of a tiger with a white beard-like tuft on its chin was immediately attributed to him.

'How come all the pathways do not run into each other, Kene?' Kato asked after he was done making his mental connections.

'The pathways are like one of your mother's shawls, Kato. Have you seen how many threads she weaves? Ever kept count?'

Kato shook his head. There were *so many* threads that went into a single shawl. They met, wove around, went under and over, yet through some strange magic they didn't end up as an unrecognizable mess. Somehow, in a way that only the weaver could know, when his mother pleated the last loose bunch of threads, what emerged was a beautiful shawl.

He felt a little sorry for the muza muza. 'Well, if you want to know,' he said. 'I am still as terrified of her as I was before.'

Kene laughed aloud. 'If you say so, if you say so. She has a story too.'

'Why was it here?' Kato asked scanning their high perch.

'Came to see the boy I chose to be my storyteller. She meant no harm, Kato. I've told you how your kind elsewhere have become too powerful and have killed rivers and mountains.'

Kato nodded.

'I've detected that the pathways are beginning to waver, and somehow it is the human pathway that seems to be causing it. I fear that more than ever the human storyteller must tell their stories with courage, because though I do not know why, if your pathway breaks it will unravel everything else.'

'Why?' Kato asked breathlessly.

'As I said, my friend, I do not know the answer yet, but I'm sure that before we leave it will make itself known.'

The allusion to the *long sleep* dropped a rock down Kato's chest.

═

'Pass me one of the thin ones, ilomi,' Kato's mother said, stretching her hand towards him.

He let the bamboo toy he was playing with fall to the ground and stretched himself like a cat. Standing up he went to rummage amongst his mother's weaving sticks and picked the one she wanted. 'Yes, that one.'

When he brought it to her, quick as a mantis she grabbed his hand and pulled him into a hug. Despite his manly bravado he started giggling when she dug into his neck with her chin. When she finally let him go they were both laughing breathlessly.

When she went back to thwacking the loom he pulled a small stool close to her and watched her at work. The intricacy of what she was weaving boggled his mind. So many threads! Trying to imagine the pathways as he saw his mother work made his mind reel. How many pathways were there? And more importantly who was the weaver? Was it Alhou the creator?

His mother was weaving an aqhumi, a shawl of significance that only grown men who'd achieved good social standing by hosting a series of communal feasts could wear. It was black, with three red stripes running down either side. In the middle were twelve shield motifs arranged in threes, equally spaced and covering the entire length of the shawl from top to bottom. Vermillion lines hedged off the sides lengthwise.

Good thread was hard to come by and his mother had recently acquired the best kind in a trade with a villager who'd trekked to Assam for salt.

'It will look good on your father,' she said happily.

Kato nodded with a smile. He would get his own shawl when he stepped into adulthood. He remembered his grandmother's gift lying tucked inside the blankets in his room and felt a flush of embarrassment travel down his chest.

'Ishou!'

He swung his head around. It was Apu.

'There you are.' His friend flopped to the ground beside him, huffing for breath. 'How are you, ani Nisheli?'

His mother took the time to stretch her back and groaned. 'We're all very well, Apu. How are your parents?' she asked. 'Haven't seen them in some time. What with the weaving and field work.'

'They're well too, thank you. I wanted to steal Kato away if you don't mind.'

Kato lifted an eyebrow and Apu shushed him immediately.

'Why, of course!' his mother said. 'He can't be home the whole day with his mother like an old woman. Take him, but stay out of trouble!'

Apu was red with pent-up excitement, and when they were finally alone he let it out in an explosive exhalation of air.

'Ishou!' He grabbed a very confused Kato's arm and leaned into him. 'My uncle has come to visit!'

Kato gave him a puzzled look. What was he supposed to make of that? And which uncle was this anyway?

'Guess what he's brought with him?'

Kato's face wrinkled in irritation. He didn't like suspense very much.

'You're no fun at all!' Apu exclaimed as they walked. 'Remember what I told you about the uncle who saw the timi-ala?'

Kato nodded.

'It's the same uncle! And he's brought with him a timi-ala's fingernail!'

Kato felt lightheaded. The idea was inconceivable, that Kene should fall to a man. But even the tiniest possibility made him want to throw up. Face pale and colourless, he began running in the direction of Apu's house without waiting to see if his friend was with him.

'Come in,' Apu entreated, but Kato just stood in the courtyard and refused to budge.

'Okay. Just wait here then,' Apu said, before rushing into the house.

Kato heard him plead with someone who he assumed was Apu's uncle. After a while he heard his friend whoop in delight.

'You better get it back to me safe,' he heard the adult voice yell, and out burst a very excited Apu, holding a small cloth-covered thing in his hands reverently. 'Here, ishou,' he said, bringing it closer to him.

Kato held his breath as Apu removed the folds, one at a time. When the thing inside finally showed itself Kato burst out laughing like a mad man. He clamped his hand over his mouth to lower the volume of his funny laughter, but he just couldn't make it stop. Apu gave him a very hurt look and though Kato felt bad about it he just couldn't stop.

It was the fingernail of *something*, that much was evident. But it was a small fraction of what Kene's nails would be, and furthermore, it was black like a monkey's. He knew now that Apu's uncle had the same fondness for tall tales like his brother and nephew. He felt like such a fool for thinking for even a moment that a human had felled his giant friend.

The hurt look on Apu's face began to change and soon enough he too was hollering loudly. 'I swear it looked more convincing in the light of the kitchen hearth, ishou.' He wheezed.

When they were truly over their mirth, Apu returned the fingernail in the cloth to his uncle. Then they went off to wander over the fragrant mountainside carrying two roast sweet potatoes, courtesy Apu's mother.

Two Months Later

15

A Curio

Kato stood back and looked at the notch he'd just made on the doorframe. The last one had been made about two months ago and the new one was visibly higher—not by much, but undeniably higher. He had grown taller. If he took after his father, there'd be several more notches before they stopped going any higher. But of course, Kene still carried him around as if he were no more than a newborn.

The giant's stories continued to awe him. When they'd last met, Kene had told him about the story of how all men had once lived together. The idea boggled his mind, for then how did people understand each other? But then Kene told him that all languages had the same mother! His wonderful stories seemed to have no end. Bearing enough resemblance, yet so very different from the folk tales of the Sumi, they had taken root in Kato and changed him, without even him realizing. His mind now reached back into time and saw the expansiveness of the human story, one that didn't begin and end with a single life or even a single people.

Where is this all going to end? He'd paid extra attention and remembered each of Kene's stories down to the smallest detail, but he was still a mute and a coward.

'Ilomi, do you want to take boiled eggs to school?' his mother asked, peering out of the kitchen. He nodded with a smile. 'I'll put in three so you can share with Apu.' Kato blanched inwardly; Apu had some of the nastiest smelling farts and boiled eggs seemed to make him particularly gassy.

Oh, well. Can't be helped. They shared everything.

'Your father and I will be at the river today,' his mother said. 'If you'd like, come down after school.'

He whooped excitedly, jumping around his mother and making a nuisance of himself. 'Enough!' she protested half-heartedly, roaring with laughter. He loved their fishing trips! *Tonight is a full moon too!* He couldn't wait for the day to begin.

'Children!' the teacher shouted, trying to get the attention of his chaotic class.

'Children!' he shouted again, so loudly this time that the class, outdone and humbled by the teacher's capacity for loudness, halted their antics and gave him their full attention.

'Good,' he said, his face a very deep shade of red from having exerted himself so early in the day.

'Today we've a guest with us.' Kato noticed the thin man sitting by himself with a disdainful look in the corner for the first time. *How odd that he can be so quiet!*

'Ishou, please come to the front,' the teacher, Aghoto, said. The thin man left his seat and came to join the teacher in a very self-important manner. 'This is Mr Jevishe, a former classmate from Impur. After our studies he was chosen because of his brilliance to translate for the white men by Mr Hutton the chief Shaha himself!'

The children gaped, wide-eyed and awed, and evidently this pleased Jevishe, for he beamed and pushed his bony chest out farther than one would think possible.

'Yes,' the teacher continued not bothering to hide his own awe, 'he has been to Kohima and Dimapur!' A stunned hush fell over the classroom and Apu began poking Kato's sides urgently with a pointy elbow. Very few of even the menfolk had been to Kohima, but Dimapur! They said that there were so many people in Dimapur that one couldn't possibly get all their names. And the train! The teacher had described it as best as he could, never having seen one himself; what the children understood was something like a giant iron caterpillar. Mr Jevishe had the classroom's undivided attention.

'Today I have requested Mr Jevishe to spare some of his precious time to talk to you about the wide world outside.' He paused for a moment here, giving his friend a meaningful look. He continued with a grin, 'And perhaps if you behave he will show you something quite wonderful!'

'Ah,' Mr Jevishe said, brushing the front of his fancy-looking coat, calling attention to it in a way that was too obvious, 'children, this little village is all you know but beyond these mountains there is a whole wide world filled with such wonders! Yes, I have been to Dimapur, many, *many* times.' The last bit he emphasized strongly.

'Right now you likely think that it is all right for you to grow here, get married, work and live your lives out. If you only knew how insignificant this place is you would do everything you can to leave and explore the world outside,' he continued. The teacher raised an eyebrow.

Kato did not like him at all. 'Puffed up character, no?' Apu whispered in his ear. Kato thought that this fellow's roots had long since shrivelled and died. In his fancy clothes, putting on airs and talking down to village kids. Is this the *change* Kene had told him about? He did not like it one bit.

'Ishou, do you see how lovely Narto is looking today?' Apu whispered in his ear again with a doe-eyed expression. Kato swatted at him irritably.

Kato didn't like the teacher's friend but even he was impressed by what the man produced out of his pocket later.

'Look at this,' Mr Jevishe said, taking out a square piece of paper the size of his palm, 'this is a photograph.' The children crowded closer to get a good look at this so-called 'photograph'. Despite his dislike for the man, Kato too drew closer to the front behind Apu. His breath caught in his throat when he saw that on the paper that Mr Jevishe was very careful to keep away from the grubby hands of the children, there was the image of a man standing. It was not something drawn but a real person—just flat and tiny, but a real person nonetheless.

'There is something called a camera with which you can make images like this of anyone,' Mr Jevishe announced after tucking the photo back inside the safety of his coat. Kato wondered that such a thing could exist. What amazing things he could do!

'A white woman was so impressed with my knowledge of English that she made me a present of this,' he said.

'Who is the man in the picture?' Apu asked. Mr Jevishe apparently did not like the question one bit and sounding offended said, 'Who knows but no Sumi I've met till today has another like it.' Kato glanced at the teacher and saw a hint of irritation there.

The teacher dismissed the class early and left with his friend. Apu and Kato hurried home to help their parents in the fields.

—

'Lay off them now, Kato,' his father said, 'too much and you know you'll have a tummy ache later.' His mother stood up from her work in between the rice stalks. 'Your father is right. Come help me over here.'

Kato finished his third cucumber, the juices running down his chin and onto his bare chest and shorts. Giving his mouth a quick wipe he inhaled deeply. The rice stalks were growing most satisfactorily and had started releasing an appetizing smell in the air.

It was a wonderful day for the sort of work they were doing. Taking small hoes that were held in one hand, they cleared the spaces among the rice stalks of the weeds. The earth was loose and fresh, and a particular smell came out of them when they were dug up. Without warning rain clouds gathered above and they had to seek shelter in the little field hut.

It was a little early for lunch but they opened their lunch packs and set to eating rice with fish roasted on open fire and boiled wild leaves. Kato wanted something to spice up the lunch and so he dashed into the rain outside and soon came with a handful of green chillies. The three of them ate silently, listening to the pitter-patter of rain on the straw roof.

'I hear the teacher Aghoto has a guest visiting, Kato?' his mother asked after the satisfying lunch. Kato nodded wishing he could tell them of the photograph. 'It is seldom that we get guests from the outside, I wonder what sort of man this friend of your teacher is. I hear that he even wears clothes like the white men do.'

Kato made a face and shook his head, indicating his dislike of the fellow. His mother laughed at his expression, 'Surely he can't be that bad!' she exclaimed.

The rain stopped after about an hour and when they went out to work again it was wet and muddy. Nisheli took corn and brinjal for her mother when they returned home later.

The next day at school Kato learned that Mr Jevishe had been seen leaving the village early in the morning. The teacher went about his business as usual but sometimes Kato would catch him grinning to himself.

Kato went with his mother to visit his grandmother in the evening. Apuza was too old to go to her field and so Kato's parents cultivated it in her stead, and gave her a portion of the harvest each year. She however had a sprawling garden that she kept full of vegetables and fruits; every season there was something or the other ready to be plucked or dug in her garden. Still, Nisheli always made a point to take some of the produce from her field to her mother whenever time allowed. Also, since his grandmother lived not far from the chief's house, she always had the best information at hand, all the latest news too.

'A very arrogant young man was brought low, my dear,' his grandmother told her daughter with amusement.

'How so, Iza?'

Kato perked his ears and carried the kitten he was playing with closer to his grandmother.

'This fellow, Jevishe is his name I believe, this fellow had a wonderful piece of paper with a man's image on it.'

'Oh! What a pity that he's left! I would have liked to have seen it too,' Nisheli exclaimed. Her mother smiled at her, 'Don't be too sad about it, daughter.'

'The chief too heard about it, and invited him for dinner—to hear about the wide world—he said,' she laughed alone leaving her daughter and Kato with puzzled expressions. Kato thought that his grandmother's queer behaviour had a most interesting reason behind it, and the suspense began to get unbearable.

'Oh! The chief killed a big rooster in his honour, and plied him with both food and flattery. "How wonderful!" he would exclaim at the man's accounts. "How brilliant!" he would say at his exploits. Then fully fed, and most satisfactorily oiled, he passingly brought up the paper.' A kind of comprehension dawned on Nisheli and she began to laugh, not so much because she knew, but because she knew enough of the chief to suspect what was coming. Kato became irritated now that he was the only one who appeared clueless. Impatiently he shook his grandmother to continue.

'The young man showed him the paper, and the chief took a long look at it. Suddenly he exclaimed aloud and started weeping! Everyone gathered there became alarmed, especially the young man because the paper was in the hands of the chief. "Oh! This is my great maternal uncle! Oh! Fate has brought you to me!" he cried.' His grandmother and mother now began to laugh and hoot in earnest; a smile began to tug at the corners of Kato's lips too.

After a good, bellyful laugh his grandmother continued, 'The young man was at a loss for words. The chief had ambushed him so perfectly that, though he suspected he was being had, there was nothing he could do. The weeping chief related a very sad tale about his great uncle who had gone missing many years ago, and the heart-breaking sorrow of his wife and children. "Thank you, kind sir!" he said to Jevishe, "it will console them to have this." And with that, without a single word in from the young man the paper was seized!' The laughter started again, accompanied by much thigh slapping and hooting, Kato joining in this time unreservedly.

'Of course, the chief wouldn't be accused of stealing, so he forced a very fat pig on the young man who was still speechless. I'm sure his arrogance was much tempered when he left early in the morning with the unwanted pig on a rope leash,' she said after a while, wiping the tears from her eyes.

'Oh mother!' Nisheli exclaimed later, 'this paper, was it wonderful?'

'Wonderful indeed, but I mistrust it. I think it captures people's souls or a part of it, and will give the owner of the paper power over them. Why, the fellow in the picture, no relation to the chief at all I'm sure, looked so sad and sorrowful that I wonder if he too knew he was being captured this way!' she said enigmatically.

'But just looking would be fine, I'm sure,' her daughter said.

'Looking would be okay I suppose,' she admitted reluctantly. Soon enough the three of them went to the chief's house and requested to be allowed to see the picture of his 'great uncle'.

'I suppose you're, right mother,' Nisheli said as they looked at the photograph, 'he does look sad.'

'Come now Kato, let's be off,' his grandmother said, 'who knows what it will do to the souls of young children.'

'You must never let anyone make such an image of you,' his mother told him solemnly on the way home. Kato dutifully nodded, but of course he didn't believe in the soul-capturing nonsense. How wonderful it would be if he could acquire a camera when he grew up. On the one hand he intensely detested what Mr Jevishe represented but on the other hand if *change* brought other things like the photograph, Kato couldn't wait to find out more.

16

Premonitions

Kato's heart sang gloriously like only a heart with a wonderful secret could.

When Kene had come to him first there was always the worm of doubt that kept nibbling at his mind. *What if he stopped coming?* After that first time when he'd concluded that his giant friend had been only a dream, only to have Kene return, the fear of Kene being a dream had been replaced by the fear of being found out for a coward and abandoned.

But now September was coming to a close, the wind had turned into a cold caress and Kene would be coming again tonight! And school was also off, allowing him the leisure of barrelling over the mountainside alone. The chief had taken the teacher with him to Kohima to pay house tax to the British government. Though the white men mostly left them alone and rarely visited the house tax was insisted upon. One rupee per house. Kato's parents had paid theirs.

A gust of icy wind sent a rustle through the tall bamboo and Kato stood still, lifting his chin, allowing the falling bamboo leaves to cascade over him. As much as he enjoyed Apu's company he needed these times alone, where he had only himself to address. He'd sought out this same spot where the men had been sent into a panic by the leopard months ago. This was one of the ways he kept the accusing voice at bay. The one that whispered *coward* and *betrayer*.

See! I'm not scared! he shouted inside as he swung his arms around.

Crash! The sound of something falling was followed by loud cursing.

Kato dropped low and swung his head around, trying to pinpoint where the sound came from. He thought he knew who the voice belonged to.

'Oh! Pity these old bones of mine!'

Having identified the position of the voice he smiled to himself and crept towards it. He knew who it was.

Ghonili, the tu-umi was struggling to get a pile of dry wood together that had fallen off her back. She groaned as she struggled to retrieve the absconding bits.

Kato watched from the shadows for a while. A few months ago he'd have made a quick escape, thanking his luck on not being seen. Today a different kind of thought trail occupied his mind.

Not too different from me. What kind of stories do you have?

She spun around when he walked up to her soundlessly and began picking up some of the wood.

She watched him retrieve all of the scattered bits silently. When he took the one in her hand a low rumbling laugh began in her throat. Giving her a lopsided smile he put the one he'd taken from her with the bundle and tied it all together with the rope she'd brought. With a heave he slung it on his back and began walking towards the other side of the mountain.

She followed behind chuckling to herself under her breath. Occasionally she'd start cackling to herself but it did not scare him.

When they finally reached her hut he let the bundle fall to the ground. It was *quite* heavy.

'Wait here,' she said before going into her hut quickly.

A while later she emerged with an old cloth and brought it to him. When she uncovered what lay inside Kato smiled. It was a couple of wild plums. They ate them together and when he finally stood to go home she patted him on the back.

'You're a good little squirrel,' she said, giving him a fond smile.

He laughed his queer laugh and began the walk back home. His heart sang once more.

——

'Today, there is no need to go very far. Let us walk around the village and talk,' Kene said.

Kato's face fell. What use was walking in the village when he'd waited so many days to get away? 'Won't people hear us?' he asked morosely.

'I assure you that not a single soul will leave their bed until I will it so,' the very sure reply came.

He looked at the giant curiously. Something was off about him tonight. He couldn't tell what it was, but he knew it as surely as he knew his own name. He followed Kene silently, knowing full well that he would tell him only when he was ready.

It was quite strange, walking through the village in the middle of the night with not another soul in sight. Seeing the village seemingly deserted was disturbing in a sort of way, as if he had been left behind while he slept. He knew that inside each house there were people sleeping, yet it reminded him of the eerie, abandoned village Kene had taken him to before, lost to time. He hurried to catch up to Kene.

They kept walking, talking about small, little things. Kene seemed very curious about what Kato had seen or learned during the time he was away. It began to seem so terribly normal that he felt as if he was walking with Apu instead of this giant out of the folktales. He imagined that it was a bright day instead of this deserted moonlit scape.

'Kene, what if all the villagers were to wake up now and see me talk? Wouldn't that be quite wonderful?' he exclaimed.

Kene gave him a cryptic smile. 'That would indeed be quite wonderful my friend, quite wonderful.'

'Kene, have you ever seen a photograph?' Kato asked him as they walked past his uncle's house.

'No, this is the first time I'm hearing of it,' Kene said sounding genuinely puzzled, 'what is it then?'

An idea occurred to Kato. 'No one will wake until you will it?' he asked.

'Yes, that is so.' Kene replied.

'Ah! Then let me show you a photograph!' Kato said overjoyed.

The chief's hunting dogs nuzzled into each other as they dreamt of whatever prey they were chasing. Kato carefully stepped over them and pushed the door to find that it opened easily enough. Inside the first room were the young boys who had taken up residence in the chief's house, as was the Sumi tradition. Not a soul stirred as he tiptoed past them further into the house. Kene being far too big to fit inside the house waited outside like a patient old man.

Quite convinced now that Kene had it right, Kato boldly walked into the room where the chief slept with his two wives and their children. The photograph was easy to locate, for where would a person keep something he took pride in but a place where people could see it. Taking the photograph out of the thatch wall where it had been stuck almost carelessly, he made for the door as boldly as you please.

'It is really quite amazing, little man,' Kene said as he looked at the little square piece of paper in his hand. He shook his head in amazement again and again. 'How terribly clever you human folk are!

'Keep it back where it was, Kato,' the giant said after he was satisfied, 'we've borrowed it without permission. The least we can do is to return it as it was.'

Though he'd seen it before Kato couldn't help himself and took a good long look at it again before he returned it. After his grandmother had said so, it became impossible for him to see the tiny man in it as anything but sad and melancholic.

'My grandmother says that it captures the souls of man, these photographs...' Kato said as they went downhill.

'Did she now?' Kene asked, 'perhaps it does in a way you and I couldn't understand.'

'Teach me a game.'

They were seated on the open ground outside the schoolhouse and the moon shone on them like a bold jewel. He peered at his giant friend. *Something really was odd.* He was sure there was something very obvious that he was missing about Kene. 'What kind of game?'

'Something that the children play.'

What am I missing? 'How about the game of five pebbles?'

Kene readily agreed. 'Yes, that sounds nice.'

He took his time finding the best five stones he could find—not too small, not too big, smooth to the touch and with just the right heft.

'Like this.' He tossed the stones off his palm and caught them on the back of his hand. Two fell off. *Tsk,* Apu was better at this. Although awkward at first, soon the unfair advantage that the giant hands had became apparent and the teacher insisted on ending the lesson.

'Is something wrong?' Kato had exhausted all his patience.

'Hmmm...' Kene rumbled. 'Will you roast me some corn?'

Kato stared at him in bafflement. 'Didn't you hear me?'

'Later, later,' he replied waving his hand. 'Will you roast me some corn?'

'But don't you eat everything raw?' he asked.

'Yes, but raw is raw, and roasted corn is different,' he said simply. Kato, still gaping at the idea, had to admit that Kene had a point.

Together, they lay down on the ground outside Kato's home and looked at the stars while chomping on roast corn. Funny enough, Kene ate daintily, fishing a few corns out with his teeth, eating like a bashful girl. Kato had been careful to cover the ashes outside with old ash so his parents wouldn't suspect a thing, though his mother would wonder about the missing corn from her garden.

'It is almost here.' Kene spoke into the vast silence. The words had a chilling undertone.

Kato shot up in alarm. 'What do you mean?'

'Do you know how many years I've lived?'

This unexpected turn put him off balance for a moment. He knew that Kene was very old, but he'd never really cared to put a number to it. 'Hundreds…?' he ventured doubtfully.

'Thousands…' Kene smiled at him with a distant look. His eyes were half-lidded, looking as though he were half-asleep.

'I've watched so many of your kind come and go, doing the things you do. Ihemu the mighty who slew the giant serpent tusa, Teli the wise woman who became chief and the songs they sang of her, Pheve who wrestled with wild mithuns and bears. I watched Khape the builder fashion his homes on the sides of cliffs so sheer that the mountain goats steered clear of them. Even your mighty Thahakhu, your vaunted mountain, I watched it come forth from the ground.'

Kato was struck speechless. He had no idea that Kene was *this* old. He knew nothing of the people Kene spoke of. They were not told in his folktales, nor were any mention ever made of them. He realized how insignificant his own years were.

'Watched them build, then destroy, then burn and ravage. And then build once more! Over and over again… such perplexing creatures.

'After a while it begins to look the same… the beginnings and the endings—all of it.' Kene paused and seemed to have lost track of things. 'Even though you've known from the beginning you almost forget… as though it were really from a dream and not real.' He chuckled to himself.

Kato peered at his giant friend curiously. It looked like he'd forgotten all about him and was talking to himself.

'It will not be the same this time,' Kene said with finality. 'I feel them. Our pathway has begun to pull away.'

Kato stared at his companion. It finally dawned on him. The giant was acting like a nervous child tonight. *Maybe even he felt fear?*

But what could scare Kene? The idea seemed bizarre.

'There are things I must do. I cannot come to see you for a while.'

Kato felt his heart skip a beat. *Was it ending already?*

Kene suddenly grabbed Kato's arms and turned him to face him fully. His eyes seemed a little mad and it scared him.

'Will you make the oath with the land tonight?' The desperation seemed to muddle his words.

Kato struggled to pull his arms free. Kene's grip hurt him for the first time ever. 'I can't,' he protested weakly.

Kene let go of his arms quickly, looking ashamed at what he'd just done. 'I'm sorry. I'm sorry,' he apologized before standing up and walking in circles. After a while he came back and stood before Kato. 'Take this,' he said urgently.

Kato looked down at the giant palm and his breath caught in his throat. The most amazing blue stone gleamed in Kene's palm. Kato forgot to breathe as he slowly took it and held it up to his eyes. It looked like a sliver of the moon itself. The blue of it leaked onto his face and he noticed streaks of white running across the blue, like many falling stars in the night. 'Is this an agha-tu?' he asked, his voice barely above a whisper.

'Yes, I believe that is what your people call them,' Kene replied. Kato looked up, surprised. The giant looked unsure, like someone who was already regretting his decision. 'Keep it away,' he said wrapping Kato's fingers around the stone quickly and looking away. 'Only when you are in danger, remember that, Kato,' he said. 'There is a consequence to using it.' Kato gripped the stone tightly in his hand and nodded. 'Only when you are in danger,' Kene repeated. 'Not for any other reason.' Kato nodded again, finding Kene's behaviour very strange.

'Now repeat after me,' he commanded. 'Kene, second after Lakhe, I have need of thee.'

Kato repeated the words carefully. Kene made him repeat it again and again until he was satisfied. 'Say that thrice and remember also that you are to use it only when alone.' Kato nodded and held up the stone to his cheeks.

Kato began a song when the silence drew out unendingly. It was the first time he was singing, and he began hesitatingly at first. As his voice became surer, he wondered why he'd not thought to sing before now. After all, he loved his mother's voice when she sang her songs, and, though he'd never sung, he knew every one of them. A song of melancholy started without any real thought,

'Ah, Love of mine, these mountains cannot contain
the love, the love that burns in my heart for you,
Ah, when you go down to the river where you are
Remember, my love, there's one who pines for you,
Dearest beloved, it is all I can do to keep living

When your going has struck me down like death itself…'

After the song ended Kato looked at his friend beside him to find him smiling with his eyes closed, what looked like a tear caught in the folds of an eyelid. 'Sing the song again,' the giant requested. Thrice he was asked to sing, and thrice he sang until the words began to mean something to him.

There was a sadness there that Kato couldn't understand, but it reached into him too. It was so unlike the song his heart had been singing during the day. Unexpectedly he found a sigh breaking on his lips. When he fell asleep the moon was still perfectly round and high in the sky.

17

Ghileqhi: Winter's Wind

OCTOBER

Kato placed the last firewood on the stack he'd been working on. Barely knee high when he'd started, it was a sizeable stack now. Stopping to rest at last, he went to his parents' bench and lay down. His nose twitched, sensing the rich, pungent axone broth broiling away even from here. *Pork, probably*, he thought, his nose picking up the tiny hints in the rich smell.

He hadn't seen Kene since their last hasty visit. In the two months since then winter had come to roost in earnest and now at all times there was fog and the ghostly mist. *Where are you, Kene?* he thought as the thin sweat evaporated from his body in the cold breeze. *I shouldn't worry*, he told himself for the umpteenth time. But the strangeness of their last meeting bothered him like a sore tooth.

Could even Kene come to harm? This 'distant rumblings' he spoke about, what could they be? Could he have gone for the long sleep? *No!*

He was surprised by his own vehemence. But how could he when there was so much unfinished business between them? The hurt he felt inside when he tried to even consider the notion was as heavy as a rock, colder than frost. *No,* he told himself again. Casting a worried eye across the late-afternoon sky he went into the orange glow of the kitchen's warmth.

The back-breaking harvest season was over and everyone in the village was languid. It had been a good harvest, and now, with the grain safely sequestered inside the granaries, there was reason to relax and allow winter to lull them. Fires had moved from inside kitchens into courtyards where they burned throughout the day, trying to push back against the unrelenting cold.

Apu came in blowing into his cupped hands. 'Aishhhh!' He rubbed them together furiously. 'Apu, how're your parents?' his mother asked from the fireside where she was patiently stripping dry venison that she'd roasted first in the hot ash.

'Why ani Nisheli, they're content and lazy like overfed puppies. I'm sure they're dozing somewhere even now,' he replied characteristically.

She laughed aloud as she pictured them in her mind. 'You're one funny boy, you know?' she said wiping the tears with the back of her wrist. Kato sniggered and mock punched him on the shoulder fondly.

'Ishou, there's been reports,' Apu whispered, looking intently at him.

Kato lifted an eyebrow suspiciously.

'I swear I'm serious!' Apu said. 'Some of the councilmen are gathered at the council hall, right?'

Kato nodded. Someone had come to fetch his father for the meeting earlier.

'There was a visitor,' Apu said with a smug look.

'Apu, stay for dinner?' Kato's mother said.

Apu's eyebrows danced in delight, 'Yes please!' he exclaimed, happily turning toward her. He loved her cooking and would find any excuse to stay for food, and they enjoyed his company, so it was a fair exchange.

'As I was saying,' he said bringing his attention back to him, 'there was a visitor, and he is why the meeting has been called. Maybe it's something to do with the iron machines that flew overhead a few times?' The uneasy feeling Kato had been nursing rushed to the surface.

The first one that he ever saw was as beautiful as any eagle—sleek, fast, and very obviously deadly. It made a sharp buzzing sound as it had streaked overhead. The teacher said that there was a person who flew it from the inside and the villagers had argued about it for days. *Evil spirit,* some said. Then another appeared not long after, this time fat and lumbering, making the loudest din. The villagers banged drums and utensils, and when it disappeared into the distance, some took it as a sign that it was an evil spirit because it had fled from them.

Kato didn't think it was any evil spirit. The photograph had told him that there were a great many things in the world he didn't understand. Yet, a sense of foreboding took root in him whenever one of these machines flew overhead. It bothered him that they just appeared without any explanation. *They must mean something,* he'd thought before. This morning he knew that Apu spoke the truth and they'd have an explanation at last. Strangely he didn't wish to know.

His father suddenly came home in a great rush and started conferring with his mother urgently. The boys immediately went closer. Noticing them, his father stopped the hush-hush speaking and raised his voice. Kato felt as though he'd been knocked over by a tree as he listened to his father. Kene's premonitions had come true.

The villagers had been hearing from the few visitors from outside that a great war was raging between their white Shahas and the people from the Far East. The Nagas too fought their many wars, but they were small skirmishes with dao and spear, and to the village folk the idea of millions of soldiers fighting with guns and metal machines was unfathomable.

'There's to be a communal meeting,' his father said.

'Now?' Kato's mother clapped her hands, sending a small puff of ash into the air. 'Maybe you can finish the cooking if it won't take much time…' his father said a little doubtfully, 'but we are to gather below the council hall immediately.' She quickly took the pot off the fire and placed it on a shelf. 'I can finish after we get back.'

⸻

'Why won't the white Shahas protect us?' a visibly terrified Jekishe demanded, his voice echoing the fear in everyone's hearts. 'Don't we obey their rules and pay their taxes?' A murmur went through the assembled villagers. Only the top half of their faces visible above the heavy shawls, they were gathered on the ground below the schoolhouse. A big bonfire blazed on one side. 'If they came with their guns and their machines these strange people would leave us alone,' he continued, earning the nods and rumbling approval of the villagers. Kato and Apu quickly climbed an uninhabited tree; many of them had children seated on branches already. Kato pulled his shawl tighter around himself.

The chief sat quietly with his knees crossed and his chin resting on a palm. 'This is unbearable! What does this war have to do with us?' Apu's father lamented, his voice close to fraying.

'If they'd just send guns and teach us how to use them, we could chase these strangers away,' Ato, the leader of the young men, complained. His cohorts nodded in agreement. Rubbing his face furiously, the chief stood up. A hush fell over and everyone strained to get closer. Kato wished he was at the front.

The chief had the full attention of the villagers and didn't have to raise his voice. 'A man came with a message in the night. The war hasn't begun in our mountains yet.' A murmur of relief bubbled across the crowd. He lifted a hand and the relief leaked away. 'It hasn't reached our mountains *yet*, but a splinter group has slipped in through the defences. The Shahas don't have enough soldiers to protect even Kohima, so we've been asked to leave and hide in the jungles, or make for the nearest British position.'

There was stunned silence, followed by a terrible uproar. The men protested in loud voices, while the women beat their chests and cried. The steam from their distraught mouths gathered like a small cloud of helplessness above their heads.

'Why should we run?' Kahoshe shouted. 'Aren't we the descendants of Yesukha, Arkha and Inakha? Those peerless warriors who made the very earth tremble?' Some of the assembled men became restless, rumbling like discontent storm clouds. 'Are our womenfolk not warriors too? Are they not feted like male warriors for their valour?' The murmuring picked up in volume. 'Why should we run?'

'I have seen what guns can do.' It was the chief. He spoke calmly but the authority in his voice cut through the commotion cleanly. 'Have you forgotten already?' The murmuring quieted down immediately. 'Our warriors are brave without a doubt, but a peerless warrior is easily cut down by a coward with one of these guns.' The long silence that followed was sad and pitiable. Everyone there knew that he spoke the truth. When the white men had come to these mountains, they'd changed the rules of war and death.

'What about our houses? What about our grains? The animals?' the disagreeable old man Futhena croaked. 'Yes, what about them?' a woman agreed from the back.

'This is terrible,' Apu swore as he shook his head in disbelief. Kato had to agree. The bickering of the adults below them sounded like a swarm of angry hornets.

The chief began to rub his face again. 'Burn them,' he said loudly. 'We've been ordered to burn the grain and chase our animals away!' The villagers gaped at each other. *Burn the grain? Chase away the animals?* What madness was this? The thought of doing such a thing not only sounded insane but was decidedly taboo, a thing forbidden. A Sumi villager endured back-breaking labour all year just so they could feed their family for the coming year; this order sounded akin to passing a death sentence. For a long time, there was just shocked silence and the occasional cracking of twigs burning in the bonfire.

'How are we to live?' Kato recognized his grandmother's calm voice.

'They've promised to pay us for our losses after the war ends.' The chief did not sound very convinced himself.

'Much good that will do us if we die from starvation first,' someone grumbled. A murmur of assent went through the villagers. 'And where is this messenger? Let *him* speak to us too!'

The chief clicked his tongue and shook his head. 'He's already left for the next village. It's not just us.'

More murmurs spread as everyone realized the scale of things. 'What mad war is this anyway?' Khaolipu's father asked, horrified.

'People of Ayito-phu,' the chief began, 'I know this has come as a shock to everyone.' The villagers nodded their heads solemnly. 'I know this seems like a nightmare…' he paused, 'but though it breaks my heart to say this, we have no choice.'

'Oizao!' someone sobbed pitifully. 'Oizao!' other voices joined in.

'Quiet!' the chief ordered. 'This village has survived wars before! Not even forty years ago we had to run to the jungles to escape the spears and daos of enemies. Does no one remember?' He looked at the assembly. A murmur of agreement came from the older folk. 'Did we perish? Did we disappear?' He looked at them once more. Kato had heard many times about the escape to the jungles. A neighbouring village had laid siege on

Ayito-phu, and despite their strategic location it was a lost cause. The attackers outnumbered them by a wide margin. The villagers had had to escape to the dense jungles, and yet many still lost their lives. This talk of something that he only knew from fireside stories, told by old folk with foreboding voices, sent chills through his spine.

'No!' It was old Futhena.

'No!' the chief exclaimed loudly in agreement. 'We will survive again. I know it will be difficult, and I curse this blasted war that is taking away our lives, this war that has nothing to do with us. But we will survive!' The villagers stood straighter, the men stuck out their chest and a steely look came into the eyes of the women.

'The world is changing, and we can do nothing to stop it,' the chief said sadly. 'All we can do is survive. That is our defiance.'

Kato remembered Kene's words and shivered. *Nothing will ever be the same.* Is this why Kene had been missing? Feeling very cold he nudged Apu, wishing to climb down to the fire. The lost look on his friend's face shook him. 'Ishou, where are we going to be tomorrow?' He looked at him with terror-stricken eyes.

Everyone scattered like frightened children following an instinctive need to be home, to be reminded of sane things and warmth. Kato waited for his parents to catch up, marvelling with macabre fascination at how quickly a languid day could turn into a nightmare. *Kene was right.*

'Kato papu, do you think the chief has the right plan?'

His father considered the question and exhaled slowly. 'I think he does. At any other time escaping into the jungles would be the correct choice, but in this winter?' He let the thought hang there. Kato agreed. This winter was proving to be uncommonly cold and surviving in the wet jungles without proper shelter would be too much for the very young and the very old. The chief had decided that they would march towards Kohima and seek protection at the first fortified village.

'What about the grain?' his mother asked after a while. 'It may not keep for very long.'

'I believe it will keep for at least a few months, and in any case, we have no other option.' They were to leave at dawn and some men had already been sent to dig the pits where the grain would be hidden. As soon as their home came into view Kato sped toward it and went into his room.

Taking his tin box of treasures from under the bed he took out Kene's stone and stared at it. *Where are you, Kene?* It was all coming apart—his giant friend was missing, and his village stared at an uncertain future. Should he use the stone and call him? He decided against it, remembering how insistent Kene had been that he use it only when *he* was in danger.

He heard his parents walk in silently, their footsteps dull and muffled. The bamboo door scraped the ground, and both sighed together sadly; there was no comfort here either. Kato took out his special shawl and wrapped it around the tin box before carefully placing it inside his satchel. 'Son,' he heard his father calling from the kitchen. 'Let's eat and be off.' There was no time to be wasted. Slinging his satchel across his body he walked to the kitchen.

―

The whole village watched as the last pit was covered with tree bark and then with soil. There were five in total, and together they wouldn't feed the village for a month at normal times. But these were a people familiar with lean times, and supplemented with the bounties of the forest, they could make it last for three. There was no question of keeping accounts; this was community property now.

Kato squatted with Apu atop a fallen tree trunk. 'Ishou, what if all of this was a bad dream and we were just waiting for someone to wake us up?' Apu asked. Kato shut his eyes. *What if this was one of Kene's sleep spells? What if they could just wake up to a different reality?* He felt breathless as he slowly opened his eyes. Five freshly covered pits and a whole melee of villagers met his eyes.

His heart sagged with disappointment. This nightmare was real.

'Hoi!'

Shocked into attentiveness by the strange voice Kato urgently looked around, trying to locate the sound. Everyone began to panic.

Metallic clicking sounds filled the air and shadowy men emerged from the trees, surrounding them quickly. The enemy that was supposed to be another day's march away was already here. And in a cruel twist of fate the villagers had quite conveniently assembled here to be taken prisoner together. The adults looked at each other helplessly as they realized the hopelessness of their situation.

They were nothing like they'd expected. When the white men had first come into these mountains the Nagas had thought them to be ghosts or strange devils, so different were they. Their clothing, their speech, and most importantly the way they looked. It hadn't taken them any effort at all to place them as *aliens*. These uniformed men who were supposed to be the enemies looked like the villagers. They looked so much like them that it came as a shock. Their uniforms looked old and unkempt, not like the ones the white men wore. Their boots were dusty and worn, indicating the distance they'd walked. And each one to a man looked gaunt and hungry, as though they hadn't eaten for days. There was something ravenous in their eyes and Kato shivered when he recognized it. And the guns! They'd never seen so many guns together—deadly looking guns that they knew carried death in their barrels.

Overcoming their initial shock, the villagers began to panic and many tried to get away. They outnumbered the soldiers five to one and the odds didn't seem so bad. With frightening speed and efficiency the enemy soldiers lifted guns to shoulders and aimed at the fleeing villagers. A rifle barked in quick succession like a rabid dog. The villagers recoiled and many crouched on the ground. 'Stop!' the chief shouted. 'We must think for everyone. If they meant us harm, we'd already be dead.' The hopeful escapees grudgingly returned to join the assembly. Their brief delusion about their numerical superiority withered away.

A wiry, strange-looking man stepped onto a boulder and began speaking. He had a small gun hanging from his hips and spoke with authority. The schoolteacher stepped forward and after conferring for some time began to translate for the strange man.

'I am Lieutenant Hashimoto Kenji, and these are men of the imperial Japanese army.' The teacher translated. 'We mean you no harm.' The captain smiled and said something warmly. 'He says that they are friends,' the teacher translated; a smirk hung lightly around his mouth. 'We will not stay long and will leave you as we found you, but we request that you co-operate with us.' Lieutenant Hashimoto walked on the pits they'd just covered and smiled pleasantly. 'As a sign of our goodwill we will leave these pits of yours untouched,' the teacher translated, 'but whatever's in your homes and your granaries we will take with gratitude for the imperial cause.'

'What a load of rubbish!' Apu swore under his breath. 'Take with gratitude, he says.' He spat angrily into the ground. A rough-looking soldier growled at him, and he quickly hid behind Kato.

He and Apu jostled for space as the men were separated from the women and very young children. 'Just co-operate with them,' the chief pled. 'They gain nothing by harming us.' He watched his mother and grandmother standing to one side of the other group. He looked at her worried face and felt his heart squeeze inside his chest. He felt a hand on his shoulder and looked back to find that his father had found him in the melee. 'It'll be alright,' he said but averted his eyes when Kato sought them.

The men were led to the schoolhouse and locked in from the outside. Apparently, this was just so that they wouldn't be tempted to run and report to the nearest British outpost. The schoolhouse was big, but it made a cosy prison for the 148 men and boys. Kato and Apu clamoured for space with the other young boys to look through the long hatches in the middle of the thatch walls that had wide diagonally spaced bamboo criss-crossing its length. The grown-ups gathered at the back with the young men and began a hush-hush discussion.

A loud commotion drew Kato's attention to the western side. Two soldiers were pushing Ghonili, who was dishevelled as usual. She'd come to investigate after hearing the gunshots and got caught too. 'Hmmmhhh!' She swung an arm trying to get their hands off. They grabbed her on either side, looking very disgusted.

Kato ground his teeth and furrowed his brows as he watched them force her ahead. He worried that they might lose their patience and do something terrible to her. For a while they disappeared under a jutting bluff where Kato couldn't see. He slowly counted the soldiers, noting their positions. The officer had left for the chief's house with the teacher and two soldiers. There were three guarding the schoolhouse and twenty or so soldiers with the women and probably as many on the lookout. *Probably fifty or so,* he thought, doing the calculations silently.

The soldiers re-emerged into view with Ghonili. 'Aizei!' she screamed, trying to escape the clutches of her captors.

Settle down. Just settle down. Kato prayed inside.

The men broke up their helpless meeting and hurried over to stand behind the boys by the hatch. Below the women began to jostle and scream and the soldiers pushed them back with their guns. 'Where's the teacher?' the chief's wife shouted. 'Someone tell them she's harmless.' 'Calm down, ipami,' Kato's grandmother implored to her old friend. But she was in a panic now and struggled even more. The heavy-set soldier who'd scowled at Apu earlier walked up quickly and slapped her. Staggering back, she lifted a hand to her cheek and spat at him. The commotion behind them quieted and in shock the soldiers too stared, losing focus for a brief moment.

Kato's grandmother stepped between two soldiers quickly and ran to where her friend glowered at the soldier. His face a mask of ugly hatred, the soldier raised his rifle and aimed at Ghonili with his bayonet. He meant to run her through! Kato inhaled quickly and felt his face flush with terror. As if in a dream, the men shouted for the teacher to come.

Kato watched with horror as his apuza came to stand before her friend. The soldier shouted at her to move but she stared right at him without budging an inch. Ghonili clung to her like a small child. The soldier turned his gun around and quickly struck his grandmother's face.

Kato cried out as he watched her stagger. Steadying herself she rose again and stood between the soldier and her friend, blood dripping from her cheek now. The face of the evil man contorted like a demon's. Some of the soldiers stepped forward to pull them away but the cruel man barked at them to stay away. A wicked look came over his face and he drew back his rifle. He meant to impale them together.

'Iza!' It was his mother. Her voice was twisted by terror, and it drove a stake in his heart. He saw her struggle to get past the soldiers, but they pushed back with their guns.

'Savages!' the chief spat helplessly.

The women shrieked and cried but the soldiers paid them no heed. Kato watched with detached horror as his grandmother faced down this monster, knowing fully well that she was helpless against the tip of the gleaming knife.

'Yamero!' a commanding voice boomed.

18

The Bargain

'*Ima sugu yamero!*' The officer had returned!

Kato's heart dropped with relief, but his eyes were fixed on his grandmother and the soldier.

The cruel soldier hesitated, his face livid with rage. His whole body shivered uncontrollably. 'Yamero Tajomaru,' the officer spoke, soft but firm. His lips curling up in a display of helpless rage, the soldier slowly lowered the rifle.

A big collective sigh of relief rustled through the men. 'Friends indeed,' someone muttered cynically.

Kato gritted his teeth. It was not fair at all. They had nothing to do with these men, yet here they were, calling themselves friends while threatening to run old women through with their knives. The helplessness he felt as he'd watched his grandmother almost get killed was terrifying. He resented the Englishmen who'd brought their war into his quiet mountains and with it these polite, dangerous men.

The officer appeared regretful about the whole thing. He snapped a few orders and the soldiers hastened to obey him. Kato's eyes were glued to the hateful man. He knew in his guts that he wasn't done with his grandmother yet. He'd seen the hate in his face when he'd drawn back the gun. He knew that he'd find a way to kill her before the night was over.

Desperately he looked around until he located the officer. Everything rested on him. The only thing keeping his grandmother safe was his presence. Following orders, several soldiers led the womenfolk uphill. Kato rushed to the other side of the classroom and jostled with the men to look out. Spouses and children called out to each other, fear and panic threading through their voices. He forced his way between two bodies and peered around urgently.

'*Ilomi!*' It was his mother. She stretched a hand helplessly towards him. Her other hand held his grandmother who smiled weakly at him. The cut on her cheek had stopped bleeding but she looked as though she was about to faint any moment. He bit his lips and fought back tears.

'Be strong, little squirrel,' she said. The line behind them pushed them along, and soon they disappeared uphill. He understood that they were to be confined in the council hall.

He ran back to the other side once more and looked for the evil man. He was supervising the building of a bonfire and his subordinates appeared to be receiving a great deal of abuse. *He means to kill her.*

'Look at him.' Apu had slipped to his side without him noticing. 'That one's evil, I tell you.'

Kato wished that he could do something. The evil one kicked at a log and shouted at one of the men. He saw the officer shaking his head in frustration and move away. Knives of panic stabbed his insides. His hope in the officer had just weakened. He would never side with a simple village woman over his own soldier even if he disliked him.

'Kato!'

He glanced around and found his father who was huddled with the grownups. He just nodded at him with a certain look in his eyes. The message was clear. Be strong.

'We must do something!' Apu hissed into his ear. He raised an eyebrow at him. *Like what?*

'Maybe we can slip out and free the men after the soldiers go to sleep.'

The fact that Apu didn't seem to be taking the situation seriously grated on his mind. Both of them knew that the plan was both impossible and foolish. Even if they did manage to slip out undetected, which was already inconceivable, there was no way that all the soldiers would sleep at the same time. He glared at Apu and the imp looked away.

A loud bang startled everyone. All the men jostled to look out. The reason became clear when some soldiers dragged a dead pig into the open ground below. 'The bastards have killed my prize sow,' Narto's father groaned.

'Friends...' the chief growled.

They watched as the soldiers quickly butchered the pig, steam rising from the warm blood of the animal. Their efficiency shocked the men into speechlessness. Kato found himself wincing as the sharp knives slashed into tendons and separated limbs effortlessly. There was no need for big daos, just the silent cleaving of edges sharpened beyond belief. Before long the carcass was quartered and hanging from a tree.

When the bonfire was lit he realized with a start that dusk was almost here. A panicked shiver ran up his spine as he looked at the setting sun. Soon his grandmother would be at the mercy of the darkness and the hateful soldier. He looked around for the evil man and found him gleefully skewering meat with a stick.

The men grumbled and complained about thieves as the aroma of roasting meat rose to them after a while. As distraught as he was, his stomach groaned sadly as the smell grew more and more enticing and overpowering. The sounds of laughter from the bonfire made the men irritable and cross. The soldiers who were on guard outside stamped about impatiently as they waited for their turn to eat.

Mist that had been lurking around like a thief pushed its way into the schoolhouse and gathered on the rafters. The room began to settle into a certain order now that their fate for the immediate future was settled. The bamboo benches were all piled towards the right side and the very old men made their place by them, while the young men and the grown adults squatted at the back and the young boys made their place in the middle. Cold air blew in through the open hatches but the warmth from so many bodies packed into the room mercifully kept them from freezing in their shawls.

I must do something, Kato thought frantically from a corner where he sat alone. But what could he do? Even if all the men should get free there was nothing they could do to rescue their women. He knew what those guns could do. None of them would survive. He recalled the bloodied face of his grandmother and gritted his teeth in frustration. The little light before dusk was fast retreating and soon there would be just the orange glow from the bonfire below and the little lamps hung outside. No matter how he looked at it the approaching cloak of darkness seemed to hide only death for his apuza and his anxieties flared like a dangerous forest fire.

Just then the teacher came with two soldiers. Quickly he informed them that to get around the problem of feeding the villagers five women were allowed to go out to cook. Likewise, ten men were required to fetch water from the spring. Five soldiers would accompany them to the spring and back. As to the matter of doing their nature's business they would be let out in groups of five, accompanied by soldiers yet again. Kato's father was chosen with nine others and they left with the teacher. Outside, darkness descended without ceremony.

'They're leaving, ishou,' Apu called from the hatch urgently.

In the light of the bonfire the officer appeared to be passing out orders, gesturing around with his hands. Kato held his breath as he picked out the cruel soldier. He was hanging back, trying to make himself inconspicuous. The officer began to walk uphill with the teacher and two of his men. Kato trembled in terror for his grandmother. The only person keeping the evil one from descending on her with fury was leaving.

The officer stopped and seemed to be thinking. Turning around Kato heard him shout. 'Tajomaru!'

Kato felt needles shooting through his scalp. The soldier did not answer at first.

'Tajomaru!' the officer called again and the evil one reluctantly came out and stood before his commanding officer. After exchanging a few words the officer ordered one of the men to hand over the lamp to the angry soldier and they left.

When he finally released his breath, he realized that he wasn't alone. Everyone in the schoolhouse had been watching anxiously.

'Thanks to that kind man,' Apu's father said. 'But for how much longer can he hold that devil back?' A murmur of concern went through the room.

He'd spoken what Kato felt. *How much longer?* While he was grateful for the officer's intervention he was under no delusion. It couldn't continue indefinitely.

If only Kene could help! He suddenly groped around for his satchel.

He realized with shock that he'd completely forgotten about the charm stone. When his hands found the satchel and the small tin box within it, he felt a moment's relief. *But it's not full moon yet.* His heart sank. Kene had never come to him under the cloak of darkness. *I must try.* There was no other option.

He frantically recalled the words Kene had taught him. *Kene, second after Lakhe, I have need of you.* He repeated the words inside until he could recall it without effort. He ached with the need to use the stone but he recalled Kene's instructions. *I must be alone*, he thought, impatience making his legs restless.

Only when you are in danger. He quickly buried the thought in his mind.

Dinner was brought: just rice and a thin porridge with taro and dry fish, barely enough to satiate their increasing hunger. Water too was extremely rationed, and they'd have to make do with just one bamboo flute for the night. It galled the villagers to see the soldiers enjoying their grain and their meat to their hearts' content. With nothing to do, they settled into silent thoughtfulness, each wondering about their loved ones and the uncertainty of tomorrow. To offset the freezing cold, they huddled together and their warm breaths filled the room with vapour.

Kato waited until it was completely dark. Once it became difficult to see, he stole his way to a thatch wall and slowly stuck his hand inside his satchel. Finding the tin box within the shawl he carefully pried it open. The stone felt warm and wet in his palm. Gripping it hard, he closed his eyes and spoke the words in his mind: *Kene, second after Lakhe, I have need of thee.* Shutting the lid, he crawled back to the others and began to wait.

―

'Wake up, little friend.'

Kato's eyes flew open. He hopped past sleeping figures and flung the door aside. Kene's dark hulking shape squatted in the dim lamplight outside. Waves of relief washed over him. He ran and hugged his knee, pressing a cheek against the warm, hairy skin. Kene was here! It would be all right!

'I wasn't sure you'd come,' he heard his voice fraying.

'Hrmmmm, hrmmmm,' Kene rumbled, sounding happy but tired. He glanced around hurriedly and saw the soldiers in deep slumber, some slumped over each other. 'Is this the change you were warning me about, Kene?' he asked.

'Yes, it is. Can't you feel it already? Nothing will be the same henceforth.'

They stood silently for a while, the enormity of what Kene had just said sending resounding echoes through his mind.

'Now tell me, why did you call me, Kato?' Kene asked.

'He'll kill her!' he exclaimed urgently. 'Please save her!'

'Slow down, my friend.' Kene reached down to pat him. 'Who exactly is going to kill who?'

Kato calmed himself and tried to explain as best as he could. Kene listened silently.

When Kato finally stopped, Kene sighed, sounding tired. 'Have you forgotten what I said?'

Kato shook his head, 'No, of course not. You said that I was to use the stone only when *I* was in danger.' Kene waited wordlessly, his stony expression telling Kato all he needed to know. 'I know that it's my grandmother and not me, but please!' he pleaded, 'you've got to help me!'

Kene just shook his head. 'Only when *you* are in danger.'

Kato stared aghast. *Why was he being so stubborn?* He knew that Kene could help him. 'Don't you care at all?' The silence stretched out. 'Why?' he asked, tears welling up in his eyes. 'Why won't you help me? Please let me use the charm. I'll give up my chance for her!'

'That's not how it works, little one. When you use the charm stone there is a consequence.' Kene placed a gentle hand on Kato's head.

'What consequence?'

'The charm stones aren't simply wish granting stones,' Kene explained. 'They sever pathways. Remember what I told you of pathways?'

Kato nodded, his face a mask of confusion. What did any of this have to do with his grandmother?

'If you use this charm stone our pathways will be severed.'

'You mean if I use this stone we will never meet again?' The blood drained from his face.

Kene smiled sadly. 'It is as you say.'

'Why did you give me the stone then?' Kato whispered, shaking his head. It made no sense at all.

'I had to make a very difficult choice, my friend. I chose what seemed best.'

'I don't understand. I just don't,' Kato mumbled.

'Kato, there's just you.'

'What do you mean?'

'You are the only storyteller I chose. 'You are the only one.'

'Why?' Kato said, the desperation twisting his face. 'There are so many others! So many others who speak!'

'There are other pathways,' Kene said, 'paths that are connected to a single person, paths with very clear destinies. These people are chosen, not made. I did not find you by accident. 'I followed the pathway to my storyteller, and it led me to you.'

Kato shook his head furiously. 'It was a mistake. You've made a mistake.'

'The pathway can never be wrong. There is no one better than you.'

Kato groaned and kept shaking his head.

'Are you ready to make your oath to the land tonight, Kato?' Kene asked after a while.

'No.' There was no hesitation. *The land will judge me and find me wanting. I will die.*

Kene shook his head sadly. 'Then, as much as I want to help you, Kato, you have a task and it is greater than just one person's life.'

Kato threw his hands up and laughed bitterly. 'You've made a mistake, my friend.'

'No,' Kene said simply.

After a long silence Kato lifted his face. 'I'm sorry, Kene,' he whispered. 'I can never be your storyteller.'

'Why?'

Kato felt his face flush with shame. 'I am a coward and a traitor. No, I am a *mute*, a coward and a traitor.' He'd kept it hidden for so long that when the words finally came, he felt both shame and relief, so much so that he found himself sobbing. 'If I try to make an oath with the land it will know who I am and I will die.' He told Kene about what had actually happened at the hunt, stumbling occasionally when the most embarrassing bits came up. He told him everything, up to the last, most embarrassing detail.

'I've known all of this,' Kene said. Kato stared at him. 'I have many friends with ears and they tell me everything I need to know.'

'Then why?' Kato stammered, not knowing whether to feel hurt or ashamed. 'Why keep the act going for so long when you knew I was never going to be what you needed?'

'Mistakes can be corrected, Kato,' Kene replied hopefully.

Kato's heart was a storm of emotions. 'No, you don't understand, you giant fool.' The tears began to flow freely. 'I have thought about it…many times. The truth is that I'd do the same thing again. I am sorry, Kene.' Because of me, your stories are lost.'

He felt ashamed. He'd betrayed his giant friend as he'd betrayed Apu. He was a coward and a traitor. Why would the land make an oath with him? Along with everyone else he'd been deceiving himself too the past months. It had been decided the moment he chose to betray Apu, yet he'd kept deluding himself that somehow he could still be the storyteller Kene wanted: And that at the end of it all he'd have a voice of his own.

The shame of his betrayal wrestled with his desperate need to save his grandmother now. He knew that there was no reason for Kene to help him now. He'd practically spit in his face and called him a fool. Yet, his love for his grandmother made him shameless.

'Please, Kene…' he begged. 'Please save her. You're the only one who can help me.'

Kene put a finger on his lips and thought for a long time. 'Kato, my friend,' he said, finally. 'I did not come looking for just *my* storyteller, but *the* storyteller. Your people need a storyteller too.'

'I'm sorry, but what difference does that make? I won't be *any* kind of storyteller.' Kato's voice deflated.

Kene peered at him strangely for a while, and finally nodded to himself. 'Will you promise to remember my stories?'

Kato felt tears well up in his eyes. 'Yes, of course I will. I'll never forget them, even if it does no good.' he said. Kene smiled and nodded with steely eyes, looking as if he'd finally made an impossible choice. 'I'll help save your grandmother,' he said.

Both overwhelming relief and sadness hit Kato at the same time, and his legs buckled underneath him. 'Are you sure?' he asked the giant haltingly.

'Yes, I am.'

'How are you going to do it?' he asked, still dazed.

'Not me, my friend,' Kene replied. 'Now give me some silence, there's someone I have to call.'

Kene walked away from him and began whispering into his cupped hands; he spoke a foreign language that had lots of pronounced S's. Kato wondered who this 'someone' was. He looked at the impenetrable fog and shivered. It still seemed like a dream. Outside their little envelope of lamplight, he saw only thick darkness. A long time passed, and nothing happened.

'Stop that, old friend,' he heard Kene say in his direction. The hair on the back of his neck immediately stood up and he felt icicles forming on every inch of his exposed skin. 'Leave the boy and let's talk,' Kene said urgently. Kato froze, unable to move at all. Something cold touched his ears and a warbling laugh began very close to him. Kato knew in his guts that it was the muza muza, and a thousand shivers climbed up his body.

There was a whoosh of air, and the mischievous spirit was away. Kato slowly turned to where Kene was, barely able to make out something that looked like an inverted cone of spinning leaves and dust the height of a tall man. From time to time, he thought he recognized something within it that looked vaguely human. Teeth chattering with both fright and the cold he felt the tip of his ear where the muza muza had touched him. It still felt numb.

He watched them confer. Kene would speak the foreign language and occasionally he'd hear the muza muza; it sounded like a little girl speaking with a pronounced lisp. It buzzed away from Kene again and again, appearing agitated. It would wander around for a while and return to the waiting Kene. Kato watched them strike some unknown deal, hoping that Kene would succeed in persuading it.

'It is done!' Kene said happily as he walked towards Kato. 'She will help us.' Kato heaved a sigh of relief. 'But she wants something in return.'

'Anything! What is it?'

'It will not be tonight, but when it's time you must give her what she wants.'

'Yes, I agree.'

Kene smiled. 'So be it!'

'Thank you, Kene.' Kato felt both anxious and relieved. 'What now?'

'We wait,' Kene said simply.

The muza muza began to buzz, tracing a big wide pattern around the sleeping soldiers. Kene and Kato followed behind with the lamp.

'What is she doing, Kene?' Kato whispered, afraid to interrupt.

'She's forcing herself into their pathways,' Kene replied, shushing him. When she touched the first soldier, he stood up and his eyes opened.

The soldier stood there unblinking, not making a single move. One by one she touched them all and soon they were all standing, looking like sleepwalkers. With every soldier within sight under its thrall the muza muza buzzed away uphill, presumably to pay a visit to the soldiers there.

Kato walked to the nearest soldier and peered into his eyes. The eyes seemed to look right past him, the expression stuck between confusion and vague terror. 'What will happen to them? Will they wake up?'

'Yes, they will once she undoes the knots in their pathways,' Kene. Kato walked to the other soldiers. 'But you could have done this yourself,' he muttered confused. 'Why did you have to call the muza muza?'

Kene tut-tutted. 'We operate differently. I can put them into a sleep spell, but it has its limits. Also, I cannot put them into your hands because that would be taking things too far even for me, and Alhou sees all.' The last part made a shiver run down Kato's body.

'She'll take them far away and make sure that they do not return.'

'She won't harm them, will she?' he asked.

Kene shook his head. 'That's not her nature. But you humans are frail so one cannot say how they'll take the fracturing of their pathways.'

Kato was aghast. 'Their officer was kind,' he said softly.

'One can only hope, Kato. That is the way with life.' There was nothing more to be said.

After a while the muza muza came buzzing down the path followed by a string of rickety soldiers. They looked ghostly in the mist and Kato felt sorry that they should be out where there was no warmth. 'Will you please let me give them their blankets?' Kato asked. Kene shrugged, 'If you wish.' Kato hurried and tied the blankets of the soldiers around their bodies diagonally. He ran up to the council hall and returned with the blankets of the soldiers there. The officer and his two bodyguards still had no blankets and Kato didn't want to go to the chief's house. He suddenly chuckled and went up to schoolhouse, returning with two Sumi shawls. Quickly he tied them around the officer and one soldier. The cruel one he left without a shawl.

'It's done,' he told Kene. The giant nodded and went to speak with the muza muza. 'Come here, Kato,' he said after a while. 'Give her the charm stone,' he instructed. Kato quickly held out the stone and a hand came out of the whirling dust and took it. It looked thin and gaunt. A stab of pity went through Kato as he remembered what Kene had told him about the spirit.

The spirit went buzzing down the sloping path into the dense fog and the soldiers jogged behind it like so many broken toys that had forgotten how to walk. It was almost as if they were led by a string held by the spirit, like a child at play.

'So, it is done,' Kene exhaled. Kato nodded silently.

'I have to go now,' Kene said. 'Remember my stories, little friend.'

Kato felt lightheaded. 'Are you leaving already?' He'd expected to have a proper talk, a last talk. There was so much yet to explain, so much to apologize for. 'Can't you stay a little while longer?'

'I'm afraid I must leave with the severing of the pathway.'

'Will you tell me one thing, Kene?' Kato said. 'Were you going to give me my voice if I truly became the storyteller?'

'If you mean whether you'd be able to speak, the answer is no. But the truth is that you already have a voice. It is simply a matter of finding it.'

Kato laughed bitterly. He began to feel very sleepy, and the last thing he heard before his eyes shut completely, as if from a great distance, was Kene saying, *'Remember there's no one better than you.'*

'Wake up, everyone!' the chief shouted. Cursing their ineptitude for falling asleep together, the men frantically blinked uncooperative eyes into wakefulness. 'Come out!' the chief's voice boomed happily from outside. Kato groped his way out with Apu and saw the villagers cautiously staring around like guilty thieves. It was not yet dawn but there was enough grey light to see. There was not a single soldier in sight, but their guns were strewn all over the place. The class bully and one of his lackeys came out complaining about their missing shawls, teeth chattering.

'Where are they?' someone asked warily.

'No need to check,' the chief declared happily. 'I followed their tracks; they've all left the village.'

Apu grabbed Kato's hand and shook him like a happy bear cub. 'Ishou! We've been saved!'

'What about our women?' his father asked.

'Aish!' the chief exclaimed sheepishly, 'I forgot all about them. Someone go wake them up and tell them we're saved.'

Kato walked with Apu in a daze. *It was no dream. The muza muza took them away.* He stumbled on a rock and nearly took Apu down with him. 'Are you okay, ishou?' his friend asked. Kato nodded, but his thoughts were far away. In the background he heard the running of many footsteps and the jubilant cries of the women but Kene's last words echoed deafeningly in his mind—*there's no one better than you.*

19

Suphuqhi

FEBRUARY

'Ishou! Ishou!'

Kato quickly ducked his head underneath the taro leaves and slunk into the fog below. 'Ishou!' Apu said again peering into the doorway.

'He was out there just a while ago,' he heard his mother tell him. Apu's shuffling footsteps paced across the courtyard and stopped for a while. 'Where is that idiot?' he heard him muttering. Kato clung to the sloping soil, feeling as though he were hiding from himself and not his friend. 'Your parents ready with your packing?' he heard his mother ask. 'Almost done, aza Nisheli, it's just that my mother will not stop crying,' he replied absently, still trying to locate Kato. 'No surprise there, my boy, I too could cry the whole day,' she said, voice shaking. 'Well, I'll be seeing you at the gates then,' Apu said awkwardly and sped away.

Two days after the muza muza had done its work, a messenger had come to the chief's house. The enemy soldiers had been found wandering aimlessly and had been taken captive without much resistance. There was no need to leave the village since the Japanese war efforts would be directed at Kohima, which lay well before Ayito-phu.

Kato didn't want to be around people, not even his mother. His grandmother was safe, and he told himself that it was all that mattered. Yet, the feeling of despair within him had grown into a dark, oily pool. For the better part of a year, he'd lived another life where he'd been a normal boy just like anyone else. And without him realizing, it had begun to leak into his everyday life. He'd begun to smile more, trust more.

No more.

'Won't you go to watch, little squirrel?' He looked up at his grandmother with a confused look. She crouched by him and placed a wooden plate with a big chicken leg near him. 'You haven't heard yet?' He squinted his eyes suspiciously. 'One of those iron vehicles will be coming soon to pick up the guns those soldiers left behind.' He chewed on the insides of his cheeks hesitantly. As much as he hated the idea of meeting anyone, this was too interesting to miss. Picking up the chicken leg he swiftly ran out of the hut.

The whole village seemed to have gathered at the open ground below the schoolhouse where two white men in uniforms were talking to the teacher. The chief shuffled around, impatiently waiting for the teacher to translate. Kato drew back further into the treeline and crouched between several shrubs, noting where his father stood with some other men. Even his grandmother and mother came after a while.

Soon several guns and boxes were gathered. The white men counted them, making notes in their small books. From one of the boxes a very big gun was taken out that needed two men to even lift it. Satisfied, they ordered everything bound and then several men began carrying them downhill. Kato followed along, hidden in the shade of the trees. The truck had made it till there but going beyond was impossible since the path was too narrow. The ridge he was following ended a little before where the action was and so he stood on his toes to get a better look.

CRASH!

'Aish!' the Chief chided someone. 'You could have asked first before letting go.' Kato stretched his neck and tried to get a better look at things but his view was blocked by the jutting edge. The villagers began to murmur restlessly and a small pandemonium broke out. Unable to contain his curiosity any longer he quietly crept to the edge.

A box had cracked open and there was confusion as too many helpful people were trying to get them for the white men. Kato recognized the little things that had poured out. The sheer number of bullets in that one box was mind-numbing. A shiver went through him as he realized what great peril this *war* had brought to their land.

'Ishou! ishou!' Apu had caught sight of him and was waving. He pretended not to notice but that made Apu shout even louder. When he started to climb up the ledge, Kato quickly dove into the trees and legged it out of there as fast as possible.

When he was beyond the fields, he heard the rumbling of the truck as it heaved away from their mountain. He wished that along with the guns and the bullets the white men would take away this war of theirs too. *Kene's distant rumblings. Where are you?*

The lizard and the tailorbird were the closest of friends, it is said. Inseparable they were and never far from each other.

One day the tailorbird came upon his friend sunning himself on a tree. Watching his friend in a state of unawares a mad thought entered his mind. 'Today I shall make merry at my friend's expense,' he thought and with that he broke off the twig on which his friend lay. Deprived of his perch, the lizard fell and hurt his belly. The tailorbird cackled in mirth as his friend rolled about the dirt in great anguish.

With this incident was a great war waged between the reptiles and the birds. When it finally ended the king cobra had been killed and devoured and the reptiles and birds would never be friends again.

Kato's mind was locked in a dizzying struggle as his mother's story ended in their ember-lit kitchen. *Which one am I? The lizard or the tailorbird?* The wind whistling in the darkness outside seemed to have accusing voices within it.

He must hate me. Ever since he'd come clean with Kene he'd also had to consider the other issue he'd been running from. Apu was the only other person who knew about his cowardice and betrayal. How could he have remained unchanged? *No, he must hate me secretly.*

'Something's happened, tell me, *ilomi*,' his mother said. 'Hmmmm...' he heard his father agree from the back where he smoked on a pipe.

He shook his head and turned away from the light where he could hide his face against her stomach.

'My love, tell me. Did you have a disagreement with Apu?' she pushed. He didn't like being pushed. 'Stay,' she implored when he sat up and tried to leave. 'Hmmmm...' his father said again, but louder, and somehow even though it was the same expression it sounded like he was also asking Kato to stay. She pulled at him and he allowed her hands to guide him down beside her.

'I'll not ask, but please, my love, I want you to hear me out.' She stroked his hair fondly. He leaned on her and nodded. 'Your father and I were so happy when you were born. You were such a beautiful baby!' Quite unexpectedly his father chimed in awkwardly, 'Crying, crying, crying and crying.' He guffawed. Kato also laughed happily along with his parents, the tension quickly dissipating.

'There's nothing I'd change about you, my love'.

Kato's heart forgot to beat for a long, agonizing moment. It was as though he were a tree and the words an axe that hewed him at his roots. It devastated him.

Why would she say that? Why would she say something that was just not true? His throat became like rock and the wracking sobs that tore through his chest was something none of them expected. He bolted upright and raced to his bed.

'Ilomi!'

'Let him be, let him be…' he heard his father tell her.

=

Kato watched the fire roar across his parents' field. He squinted his eyes and licked his dry lips futilely. The oppressive heat was being fanned to dangerous levels by the cold wind and he and his father had their hands full trying to keep it in check. The flames took the weeds and the remnants of last year's crop greedily. Great orange-colored tongues flicked into the fog of January, transforming giant patches on the mountainsides into barefaced desolation, leaving only ash and soot.

He'd laboured for several days with his parents to clear the circumference of the field so that the fire would be contained within the circle. Kato looked down at the fog-covered trees in the lowlands below and inhaled one long shaky, smoke reeking breath. It was eerie how quiet the mountainside was, with the only sound being the roaring of the flames and the desperate cracking of twigs and branches as they gave way to the consuming power of what prowled their grounds. He suddenly felt cold despite the heat and hunched his back, making himself smaller.

His father was further down, walking the periphery with a dao just in case a stray tongue of fire reached for an unintended section. His parents were very concerned for him. He knew because he'd caught them talking about it in hush-hush tones when they thought he wasn't around. He'd kept to himself since the Japanese soldiers, and his mother thought that the fright had sent his soul scurrying away and it had become lost. *Maybe it's true*, he thought. Maybe a part of him *was* lost.

He glanced towards his right and spotted three distant shapes working like his father and him. Apu, his father and his older brother Toito. A sharp stab of pain lanced through his heart. They'd not met since Kene's last visit. Apu *had* been by his house one more time since that time with the truck but yet again he'd hidden.

A few days later he'd gone to their hideaway under the bushes to get away. The place was overgrown with creepers, but the entrance was easy to spot for him. Just as he was about to dart into it he heard voices from inside. It was Apu with two other boys. 'Never knew this was here all these years!' a voice exclaimed. It was Ilhopu, the lackey who'd been excluded from the bully's gang after running away when they were picking on Kato. 'Quite amazing, no?' Apu said, sounding very pleased.

He didn't stay any longer. There were other friends now, and why not? *I would also choose someone who didn't betray me.*

'Son.' He jerked awake from his thoughts and found his father waiting for him with his basket on his shoulder. He followed him home with a heart that was as desolate as the field they left behind them.

20

Ghixuqhi: Planting Season

APRIL

*B*_{*oom!*}

All four of them ducked their heads instinctively even though they were inside the house.

His father swore under his breath and growled menacingly. Kato felt his heart hammer inside his chest and his eyes darted towards the others. His mother and grandmother looked terror stricken in the light of the kitchen fire.

Boom!

A louder one followed after a while.

'Do these devils not even rest at night!' his grandmother cried. Once again there was uneasy silence.

There was no need for double-guessing—the war *had* reached their mountains, ominously announced by the terrible droning and explosions that had started a few days ago. Kohima was far but this was a land of mountains, and what seemed far by foot was not very far for the eyes, or the ears.

For a people still in awe of the simple rifle, the bombs, cannons, the roaring fighter planes and the endless machine guns sounded like the end of the world itself.

Kato's mother groaned painfully as another round of explosions began in the distance. This time it sounded like the distant *plop* sound stones would make in a deep well. When it first began the villagers had been so terrified that they'd gathered outside the council hall, seeking some sort of comfort from the chief who they expected to know about these terrifying sounds. But to their dismay no matter how sure he tried to act, everyone could see that he didn't have a clue either. The schoolteacher wasn't with them any longer. He'd left with the truck along with a few of the young men who wanted to participate in this new 'war' that could swallow entire nations. For the villagers it seemed as though they had left on a journey to the land of the dead and their return was as uneasily awaited as the return of ghosts and specters.

After a day or two the villagers slowly began to act like ghosts. They seemed to have withdrawn into some place inside and in their place left slow-moving, empty-eyed, limp-mouthed pretenders. The terror had subsided but so too had the quality that makes people vital. So they appeared to carry on as before, going about their regular chores, tending to their fields, grazing their animals. Old Futhena began building a tall hut that had no obvious use, and no matter how much his daughter scolded him he kept at it, most uncharacteristically quietly. Along with the booming occasionally puffs of smoke would go up in the air in the far distance and the villagers would pause in their fields to look with detached unreality, as though the land of nightmares had somehow become visible. But this was not another world, and they were not simply dreaming.

The wind would occasionally carry the smell of gunpowder and death, and the villagers would again blink their eyes a few times and consign them to uneasy forgetfulness. They were simply going through the motions of living.

Steam lifted into the air as Kato poured warm water down his cold, aching body. The little cuts and nicks on his body from the work stung as the salt in the water seeped into them. Despite the raging war just a few mountain rages away, the land *had* to be worked, or it would pay them back in bellyache and hunger. He grimaced. A particularly nasty gash on a toe began to throb like a bee sting.

It made no sense at all. *Remember, there's no one better than you.* Kene had been very clear that a storyteller was someone special. What had he said? *A storyteller is not just anyone.* No, a storyteller was a truth teller—a courageous, truthful keeper of the land. And what was he? Kato shook his head and huffed in disgust. He wanted to laugh at Kene's foolishness but shook his head and sighed instead, realizing with a start that the water had long since cooled. Something terrible hurtled through the air with a deafening sound and then came a crash and after a while a boom that shook the mountain's very roots. Kato's skin prickled immediately with terror.

For half a minute he stood open-mouthed as cold water dripped from his hair. The sound had come from the windward side where the fields lay. His parents! Stopping only to put on his shorts he ran.

His heart pounded in his ears and the stinging cold made his eyes water, but he didn't stop—not when his lungs caught fire, not even when his limbs turned to tree trunks, he ran as though his life depended on it.

He smelled the smoke before he saw the wreck. Huge clouds of soot-black smoke billowed into the sky like pillars of doom. The closer he got the more obvious it became that the fire blazed somewhere close to his parents' field. It became clear that something was terribly wrong when he saw the faces of a few villagers who were already there.

His horrified mind struggled to comprehend what it was seeing. Some monster had gouged the land and left a furrow in it that was as ugly as it was terrifying. It started at the top of the ridge and etched a ruinous line down the slope to his parents' field. In a crater the size of a large pond sat a blazing, smoking, twisted pile of metal. Where were his parents? There were villagers gathered at the ridge, a safe distance from the smoking heap. Kato jerked his head around, trying to find his parents, but they weren't there. He ran down to the field and peered past the smoke.

'Kato!' It was his father. He turned westwards toward the river, following the sound of his voice, but his relief was short-lived; his father was alone. Reading the expression on his face Kato dashed down towards the flames. 'Stop him! Lhokashe! Call your boy back!' the chief shouted. But he was too quick for any of them.

He coughed as the smoke reached into his nose and mouth like dirty fingers. His father breathed hoarsely beside him and together they stepped into the pillar of black. It was one of the flying machines, lying in a burning heap, plumes of the blackest smoke rising from it into the sky. Behind it the resting hut miraculously looked untouched, except for the roof that had been blown away. They both spotted the fallen figure at the same time. Tears streaming down his face Kato groaned in anguish. Iza! Iza! Iza!

Stumbling to her, he retched. Whatever burned in the wreckage was fouler than foul. His father reached them a second later and together they hauled her body out of the smoke. Both lightheaded from inhaling so much smoke they staggered like drunk men and half carried half dragged her out of the pillar of soot where they met some men who'd also gathered the courage to come down. Kato felt her limp form sagging as they took her from him. *Please don't die! Please don't die!* The thought raced through his mind again and again. His legs gave way and he collapsed to his knees. A small stretcher was hurriedly constructed with fresh-cut branches, and they bore her away to the village.

Kato's world reeled when he tried to stand up and go with his mother. Iza! How long had she lain there? Someone caught him with gentle hands, and he was slowly made to lie down. 'Stay down, fellow!' Khaolipu's father commanded someone. Ipu, Kato thought. 'I, I... need... to...' His father's voice was twisted with terror. 'Quick! Water!' Narto's father shouted in a panicked voice. The cold wetness that trickled down his face and wet the earth, staining his body with streaks of brown and dirty black, cleared his mind enough that he could walk with help. Slowly he and his father followed along.

They caught up to the stretcher at the village gate. His apuza also reached them at the same time. *'Oishe! Oishe!'* she cried helplessly as she caressed her daughter's pale face all the way to their hut. His mother groaned occasionally but otherwise remained motionless. As soon as they got her inside the women took over and all the men, Kato and his father included, were chased out. They spent the next hour cleaning her, examining every inch of her body, and changing her. His grandmother finally came out looking tired and began talking to his father in hushed whispers. Kato watched, inhaling shallow breaths as his father's head drooped lower and lower. His world was caving in and he didn't know what to do.

—

Kato watched by the thatch wall as his grandmother took a wet cloth and carefully cleaned his mother's face, back, hands and legs. Since the accident she had been meticulously cleaning her like this twice a day. Pain was written on her face as she remembered what it was like to care for a child once more.

It had been three days since his mother had been *struck down*. The ruins of the crash still lay in his parents' field, hulking like the carcass of a foreboding monster, promising ruin to whoever dared to move it. 'It is the soul that's gone away,' they said of his mother. Not a single mark had been found on her, not a single wound. Yet, she lay motionless, breathing but still and unresponsive.

'Did you catch the rooster, little squirrel?' his grandmother asked.

He nodded, gesturing towards the kitchen.

'I'll be done soon. You can wait outside if you want,' she said. He sat without moving, watching his mother's chest rise and fall in an alarmingly slow rhythm.

'Very well, you may stay,' she said, pausing to look at him seriously. 'Very important work we have. I hope for all of our sake that it goes well.'

Kato ground his teeth and felt tears welling up. He looked away.

'You must be brave my love,' she said and went back to what she'd been doing.

He watched his grandmother carefully wipe his mother's eyelids with a delicate cloth-covered fingertip. They fluttered as though she was trying to wake up. In the past three days, she'd not opened her eyes once, not said a single word. His laboured heartbeats began to careen out of rhythm.

'Hoi,' a voice came from outside. He bolted upright. 'Hoi,' his father responded from the kitchen. 'Do come in.' He recognized the voice; it was Apu's mother. Several footsteps shuffled into the kitchen. *Apu must have come too*, he thought. Without waiting further, he used the window to escape.

'*Kato!*' his grandmother hissed behind him, but he'd already dropped out of sight. On all fours he silently slunk away into the garden. Several villagers had been by the house to visit. Each one brought a chicken, some eggs, eel… anything that would make her stronger. After the first visitors Kato never stayed because they all stared at him as though they expected to see something new in him. He especially wasn't going to stay and meet Apu.

He lay on his belly in the dirt under the taro plants, where no one could see him. When Apu came to the window he instinctively ducked lower. He shook his head with disbelief when he realized that Apu seemed to have actually grown a little! Looking sad, Apu looked around, sighed audibly and walked out of sight. They left after a while and Kato went back in to his disapproving grandmother. "How very rude of you," she scolded.

'Kato,' his grandmother said, 'you must not let your sorrow through.' He walked with the rooster behind her, listening intently to every word. 'She is scared, and we must guide her home. She won't come if there is anything but comfort and love in our hearts.' He nodded but his heart fluttered. Why did it have to depend on him again? The anxiety took hold of his heart, and he couldn't help but shiver as he walked. His father followed behind silently.

The sight of the blackened ruin made them all slow their pace. They hadn't been back after that fateful day, and for his grandmother this was the first time. 'My poor daughter, my poor daughter…' she whispered, her voice wilting. The twisted metal sat like a corrupted tumor in the ugly crater. Kato felt his father's hand on his back.

'The rooster, little squirrel.' His grandmother held out her hands. Kato carefully passed it over, making sure that he did not let go until it was firmly in her grasp. 'Remember you must reach out with love and comfort in your heart.' They walked together to the open wound in the land. His grandmother gently petted the rooster. 'May you be enough,' she half-whispered. They stopped when they came to the resting hut, still untouched save for its missing roof.

'Take this then,' she said, 'and in return send back the soul of the one who was lost.' She walked around the field with the rooster held out in front of her, paying particular attention to places that could be used as a hiding place: behind the granary, where the trees grew, where grass was thigh high. Kato imagined his mother's spirit crouching like a little child behind one of these places. *Come, Iza, I need you!*

'Take this then, and in return send back the soul of the one who was lost.' His grandmother made another circle. Kato and his father stood by the granary watching her calling back the soul of their mother and wife. 'Take this, you hear, this rooster spotless and perfect, and in return send back the soul of my daughter who was lost.' Kissing the rooster on the head she sent it into the open and it took off into the grasses, cackling with joy at being granted its freedom.

She came back to them, smiling. The rooster had gone into the grass without changing its course once—a good sign. 'Go on.' She nodded gently to her son-in law. Kato's father carefully walked to the spot she was in before, his face overwhelmingly tender. *She must come!* Kato thought. Going down on one knee he waited as if for a child to clamber on his back.

'Worry not my love, it is I,' he said softly. 'Come to take you home. It is I.' He repeated the words again. Kato felt the tenderness in them, the longing for his mother. After several coaxing repetitions his face changed from one of questing to one of joy, then to one of vague confusion. He stood up with his hands interlocked behind his back, like one carrying a person. Wordlessly they began the walk back home. At no point were they to make any commotion or loud noise for then the spirit would once more run away, and this time, flee even further. Kato prayed that no plane would choose this time to fly over the village. His grandmother walked ahead to tell anyone they met about the nature of their mission so that they too would show consideration. A distant *plop* nearly sent him into a panic but his father walked on without any change in his demeanour.

Kato went into their house behind his father and grandmother. The strangeness of it all wasn't lost on him; while his mother laid breathing feebly on the bed all of their attention was focused on the invisible spirit that rode on his father's back. 'Go on then,' Lhokashe said, crouching down gently beside the bed. Clutching his apuza's hand with everything he had Kato watched his mother's face intently, checking desperately for any visible sign of change. 'Go on, you're home,' his father coaxed the spirit. His mother suddenly groaned, and her eyelids fluttered open. Kato rushed to her side. The eyes opened. 'Little squirrel,' she said weakly. Kato blinked back tears and hugged her tight, feeling as though the world had fixed itself once more. His mother was home.

'What is it?' his grandmother whispered to his father later in the kitchen. Kato had just left his mother in her room. 'Hmmm…' he simply said and shook his head. 'Lhokashe, your wife has returned, and yet you've been looking troubled the whole time. Don't just shake your head and grunt like that.' He seemed to be thinking for a long time as he puffed on his pipe. Leaning back he stretched his feet out.

'It may be nothing.' He hesitated.

'Just speak your mind fellow,' his mother-in-law ordered.

'The spirit was too light. Almost as light as a child.' He swallowed hard. 'What if only part of her returned?' He turned his face to them, looking as if he was about to cry.

21

The Ghost That Everyone Forgot About

Kato grimaced as he felt his right feet sink into soft mud. The momentum of his run kept his body moving forward but his feet remained stuck and his ankle took the brunt of it. Mercifully he found that it had remained intact and he sat beside the bank to catch his breath. The cold, wet embankment offered him no comfort but he wasn't looking for anything warm or comforting down here by the river. He'd simply needed to run away. He pressed his body against the sloping soil and closed his eyes, feeling the coldness seeping into his skin, imagining himself as the ghost that everyone forgot about. For days now the terror had driven him all over the mountainside and down here to the river. He just couldn't bear to stay at home for a long time anymore.

The sound of splashing made him jerk up. Very carefully, he peered out from behind a boulder. It was his old friend the otter. Making sure that there was no one else around, he ambled over to it.

It looked at him and went back to whatever it had been doing. He stopped well before the sandy bank and crouched down. There was something in the current that the otter was trying to bring ashore but it kept failing. He sat watching it trying and failing, trying and still failing. It seemed to be something big and round but light enough for the otter to keep turning it over itself. His curiosity got the better of him and he stood up and walked over. The animal hissed, showing him little, sturdy-looking fangs, but when he kept coming it dashed into the river and swam to the other shore. It was wedged into a nook between two rocks and came out easily enough when he lifted it. He recognized the metal things that the white soldiers wore on their head when they'd come to collect the guns. This one though had a nasty-looking hole that went in at the front and came out jagged and wicked at the back. A shiver ran up his body.

He felt sorry for the river. There was nowhere it could run to. He glared down at the offensive thing for a bitter minute and flung it away from the river with all the strength his thin arms could muster. The otter on the other side gave him an annoyed look before darting into the foliage. *For you at least, nothing has changed.*

His ears perked up suddenly and he spun around. He'd heard the faint sound of warbling laughter. It sounded familiar yet foreboding. But there was nothing around, except for sand and flowing water, no place for a mischief maker to hide. *Must be just the wind playing tricks on me.* He held in his breath and listened. There was nothing. For a very brief moment he'd thought that the extraordinary had come looking for him once more. Hanging his head down he sighed and began the walk back home to his sick mother.

'Come here, little squirrel,' she called, motioning to him with a feeble hand. He did not move from the corner, brooding like a dark cloud. She smiled tenderly. 'It's okay. Come here.' Slowly he walked to her bed, allowing her to take his hand and caress it. 'Do not fret, ilomi. I'm here, aren't I?' He chewed the insides of one cheek and sat down beside her. She snuggled into his back, giggling happily like a little girl.

He lifted a hand and gently placed it on her arms. His face remained hard and tense. It had been more than ten days since they'd gone to fetch her spirit back, and though she sat and talked with them, smiled, laughed and told him her stories, there was something not quite right. It disturbed him. It felt as though she was just visiting and the time for her departure was drawing near, her hold on life so tenuous that he sometimes thought he could see it vibrating like a taut spider silk. It made his waking hours insufferable and filled his nights with nightmares.

Why?

Why couldn't they bring back all of her? Did he scare her spirit away with his need? His fear and doubt? There was something wrong with him. He knew it. Something broken. No matter how much he wanted or tried he couldn't seem to attract joy and happiness. It was always disappointment and failure. Kene was gone and now his mother too was only *half* here.

'Ilomi.' He started with surprise when he found her sitting up beside him. She reached out a hand and wiped something wet from his cheek. 'It's okay, my love. I am here, aren't I?' He nodded and kissed her forehead, feeling like a liar once more.

The coughing began: dry, hollow, and desperate. His mother frantically felt under her pillow and covered her mouth with the rag she drew out. His grandmother immediately rushed into the room, and though she never pushed him aside, somehow in the way women are good at, he found himself standing to one side as she busied herself with his mother. He walked out with frost in his heart. He knew about the foamy blood she'd been coughing up for days now.

Half-blind with grief he staggered to his parents' bench outside. He rubbed his eyes and cast his eyes over the mountainside. The realization that spring had begun to manifest over the mountains startled him. In these times of disquietude even the changing of seasons happened quietly as though it were a shameful secret. *Please don't let her die,* he thought, addressing whichever spirit would take pity on him. *What will I do without her?*

Tearing his tortured gaze away from his feet he glanced up at the sky. A plane buzzed like a busy beetle in the distant western horizon and another emerged from the sun's glow behind it. With all the ominousness of two swallows at play they disappeared into the blinding razor's edge between the mountains and the blue sky. There was a bright orange glow and one plane re-emerged and disappeared into the east again. Kato waited and a moment later a miniscule *boom* followed. It had become so predictable now. It scared Kato to think that within just a month Kene's *terrifying change* had already become so routine.

Everyone knew that death was being doled out like an indiscriminate giver's gifts just a few mountain ranges away; that corpses were piled up by the hundreds and thousands; that a single *boom* could mean a hundred dead. Yet somehow the villagers still found the fortitude to preserve parts of their life that afforded 'normalcy': Planting seeds that wouldn't sprout until weeks, pounding paddy that would be eaten months and years later, laughing, lifting their hands in greeting. It infuriated him. Did no one else recognize that everything was changing? Everything was changing, yet his grandmother still sat with her weakening daughter, laughing as if nothing was amiss. Everything was changing, yet his father still grinned to himself as he cleaned a rooster for his wife's soup in the kitchen. What about him? He knew what they seemed to not know or care about. How should he behave knowing that his mother, his *voice*, was being drawn away to the land of the dead?

What will I do without you, iza?

The pounding of his heart quickened, and his mind felt like it was coming apart. Forcing shallow breaths into lungs that seemed to have shrivelled to the size of little pebbles he stared up at the familiar hay roof, his damp, shallow breaths hot against his lips. The sadness and uncertainty he'd been carrying for weeks now became fiery fishlings that swam up his chest, suffocating him.

While struggling to draw in one more breath a thought took his mind over like the bloom of a summer fever. *I am going mad, really and truly mad. Like people said.* The terror that followed the thought made his skin break out in a cold sweat and he felt blood chilling numbness. Chest heaving like a great fish out of water he bolted upright and did the only thing he could. The one thing he'd always been good at. He ran.

Between the rhythm of his feet pounding the hard earth and his deafening heartbeat he could hear nothing else. There was someone at the village gate who stopped and seemed to say something when he raced by her, but it seemed like a dream rather than something real. The scab in the land became visible and he stood huffing on the ridge with his fists balled into tight knots. He was startled when a fat droplet struck his nose with all the conviction of a righteous cause; the sunny day had become grey and overcast without him noticing. Then the downpour began. The wet soil clung to his feet and slipped in between his toes, making every step downhill seem like a commitment. His anxieties alone had been driving his feet all this time but when he saw the resting hut he knew why he was there. The beating of his heart slowed and he walked the rest of the way feeling strangely calm. He followed the path his grandmother had taken that day, only instead of the rooster he imagined himself holding out his heart in his hands. '*Take this...*'

Blinking back the rain he plodded on slowly, coming close to losing his feet in the slippery mess again and again. *You must not let your sorrow through*. He tried to think of comforting things, things a scared child might be drawn to.

I've come to take you home, iza.

He hesitated when he returned to his starting position. Clicking his canines together a few times nervously he went on the same route again. Just to be sure. The second round done with, he reconstructed what had happened that day and knelt where his father had. He'd never done this before, but he knew that one was supposed to feel the weight of a person on one's back. He waited. His hands ached with the need to feel his mother's weight in them, so that he might take her home with him. So that everything would be okay once more. He waited. '*Iza, please...*'

The rain beat on him. Nothing happened. His tears mixed with the rain as he knelt there motionless. '*Iza, please.*' Nothing happened. '*Please, please, please...*' His heart broken he slowly lifted his head.

The ugly monstrosity rose before his eyes.

He stared at the hulking wreckage with malice. The torrent lashed his face. All the anger he felt at his helplessness, all the frustration that had simmered inside for days, all of it came rushing out.

This thing had taken his mother from him.

'AAAAGHHHH!'

He grabbed a stout branch and ran down into the crater. One foot missed its mark, the other followed in an upward arc and he slid down on his behind. Finding his feet once more he faced the twisted wreck with dark eyes, and then he began to attack it with all the strength he could muster. *Thud! Thud! Thud! This evil thing!* His feet sloshed in the rain that had begun fill up the hole, and he nearly lost his footing once more.

'Aaaaaaggghhhh!' The thuds began again with renewed energy. The shock of the impact on metal ran up his palms, into his wrists and up his arms. Soon he felt numb from his shoulders down to his fingertips. When his strength finally ran out, he dropped the splintered branch and stood there huffing. The wreckage still stared at him implacably. Overcome with helplessness against this *change* that regarded him with indifference, as though he was nothing more than an ant, he felt fear. He climbed out of the hole on all fours hurriedly. Exhausted, he lay back on the earth and screamed his vehemence at a fate that conspired against him at every turn, even as the rain rushed into his mouth like a torrential flood. In the distance another barrage of bombs made a tiny cacophony.

'Where were you?' His grandmother fussed over him, trying to get him as dry as she could. 'You shouldn't do this, you hear?' He let her continue her work. 'Don't you go adding to your mother's woes and your father's worries.' He exhaled loudly and reached for the kitchen door.

She gripped his wrist and stared at it, feeling the gauntness of it. 'I'm sorry, little squirrel...' Her voice broke and she took a deep breath. 'We've all been worn thin. Please, for her sake, eat well even if I can't watch over you always.'

He nodded and pushed the door in.

'There's someone here to see you.' He was already inside and saw Ghonili the tu-umi looking at him from the fireside. He felt like he was frozen to the ground. *Why is she here?*

She looked at him with her piercing eyes, an undecipherable look on her face. The glow of the firelight made her look different, as though she were from the past, much younger. He waited for her to speak. She had a scar on her cheek where the soldier had struck her.

'Come here, *little squirrel*.' She gestured to the low stool beside her. He hesitated.

'Go on, Kato,' his grandmother gently nudged him from behind. *Not very different from me*. Clenching his jaw, he went and sat by her. Silently, both of them looked at the fire.

'Will you give us some time alone, ipami?' she asked.

'Of course,' his grandmother replied, sounding a little surprised. She left them alone and went to his mother.

'You cannot keep her,' she smiled sadly, her voice just loud enough for him to hear. His heart raced and his breathing became laboured. He felt anger rise in him.

'I may not be able to see everything,' she said. 'But I see enough.'

Kato glanced at her sideways. She continued to stare into the embers, a distant look on her face.

'I've known it since you were a baby when I cured you.'

'You were close to death—weak and dying, barely alive.' She paused. 'Your flame flickered, and then I saw it.' Kato stared at her. *She sounds like Kene.*

'I don't know everything,' she said. 'But I felt the waves of your pain earlier and I saw it once more. Stretched taut, almost breaking.'

'Choose well. For her and for yourself.'

Kato could not understand anything. A choice? His mind was already reeling after the ordeal of the day, and he could not make sense of all this.

'You can't keep her.' She rose and left without another word.

He dreamt of Kene. They were in a big, open field. Seeing him, Kato felt the stirrings of hope in his chest—*Kene* was here! The one who could change things was here! He ran to his friend, shouting his name, but Kene didn't turn with joy or act surprised, not even when he stood in front of him. He didn't even appear to notice that he was there. *Perhaps a mistake has been made.* Perhaps instead of becoming invisible himself, he'd cast the charm on Kato. *If he hears me, that will be enough,* he thought, but as much as he yelled and shouted, the giant just didn't hear. *Kene, Kene, Kene,* he cried helplessly, and without knowing why, he started calling his mother instead, *Iza, Iza, Iza.*

He woke up with a sharp pain in his wrist. Wincing he grabbed his hand where it had hit the bamboo post. *Knock knock*. His head twisted in the direction of the door. *That was a knock!*

Knock knock. He threw the blanket aside and leapt out of his bed. Kene had come!

22

The Last Reckoning

There was no one there.

His heart sank. *What a fool I am!* Bowed over with disappointment, he was about to shut the door when a soft glow coming from the left end of the house halted his hands. Stepping into the darkness he saw a small boy warming himself by a small fire. He rubbed his eyes and blinked again and again, sure that the scene would disappear like an apparition from one of his dreams.

'Come and sit by the fire, my friend,' the boy said, looking at him with a mysterious smile. In a moment of shocked comprehension Kato knew it was Kene. But how? Why was he in the form of a small boy? He wore nothing, save for a loincloth and a belt.

Speechless, Kato walked to the fire, his mind in a daze. The boy was very small, as small as a five-year-old, and though he looked nothing like the Kene he knew, the eyes were the same. There was in them the same kindness, the same patience, the same knowing; the same ancient eyes looked at him from the face of the little boy.

'It's not a full moon night.' Nothing else came to mind.

Kene chuckled, 'It appears you are right.'

'How?' Kato asked, giving in to the amazement once more. 'I mean, why do you look like this?' He spread his arms towards Kene. It felt like the first time they'd met.

'The price for coming to see you one last time,' Kene replied. Kato was horrified. *Why?*

'There's a final lesson,' Kene said. 'There's also the matter of a debt.' He looked at him with a fond smile. 'How have you been?'

Kato's mind reached back into the recent past and the gloom came like a storm.

'Everything has changed!' He stared at Kene with haunted, sunken eyes. What more could he say? 'You were right, Kene. The mountains are burning, people die like insects. The land is being gouged and splintered as though to erase its memory.'

'I know.' Kene seemed tired, worn as an old thread. 'Those things that fly with men inside, I now know that they are the reason why the pathways have begun shifting.'

Kato understood that he was talking about the planes. 'How?' he asked.

'Those things are half man-made and half spirit. In the natural order of things, birds alone should fly, but when your kind made these things the order began changing. Your pathway grows stronger and has begun to influence other pathways. For what purpose, Alhou alone knows. If your storytellers should fail and your roots become corrupt everything else will die with you.'

Kato thought about the wreck that sat in his parents' field like a tumor, and he immediately understood what Kene meant. One of them had changed his own life so drastically.

'My mother is dying.' Kato said. He didn't know what he expected Kene to do. Offer to save his mother, or suggest a cure, or even ignore his words. However, the look of compassion he gave him drove a stake through Kato's heart. 'You didn't come to save her.'

Kene shook his head sadly. 'It is her time.'

Kato shook like a leaf in the wind, fighting back tears. 'It's not fair!' he whispered shaking his head. 'I have nothing to do with this war they speak of, and yet why do I have to lose her?'

Kene reached out a small hand and held his arm. 'Those missing people at the old ruin I took you to, they too lived like us once...' Kato's mind reeled. Iza!

'Was it my fault?' 'Am I the reason why only half of her came back?'

Kene looked at him, aghast. 'You seem to have the wrong end of the matter, my friend,' He took both hands and turned Kato's teary face towards him. 'She was never supposed to come back.'

Kato stared at him with a blankly.

'*You* were the reason,' Kene whispered. 'Her love for *you* was why she tore half of herself and came back. It is her love alone that is holding her here now.'

Kato hid his face in his palms and a tiny waterfall trickled to the ground. . She'd come back for him. There wasn't much more he could ask of her. He recalled the helpless coughing and the pink foam.

Kene waited for a long time, allowing him to take it in. The sound of the bamboo wind chimes on rooftops was the only thing that could be heard.

'Why was I born without a voice, Kene?'

The little giant looked at him wordlessly.

'If I had a voice I could have told her that she needn't worry about me.' The sobs broke his words into little hiccups. 'I…could have told her I love her… that I won't ever forget…her.'

'Is that all you want? A voice?' He sounded disappointed.

This time it was Kato that looked on in tearful silence. *Is he mocking me?*

'I'll give you my voice for good, to keep.'

Kato stared openmouthed at Kene.

'You can have it. I will become the silent giant. But understand this, it will never be truly yours.'

Anger began mounting inside Kato. 'What else?' He spoke through gritted teeth, sure that there was more to it.

'Or you can choose to learn your final lesson, be free of the terror you carry. If you choose this, you shall never speak.'

'Why are you telling me this now?' The words came out hot with vehemence. 'Just when she's about to leave me.'

'Choose.' That was all.

'Why are you telling me this now!'

There was only silence. *Choose.*

He clenched his jaw and stared into the fire. It angered him because Kene knew he wasn't the same Kato anymore. A year ago he'd have chosen to take the voice without a moment's hesitation. He'd have thought it would fix everything that was wrong in his life. But now? The world he knew was being torn apart, his mother was being tortured by her worries for him. 'There's nothing I'd change about you,' she'd said. And he'd run away from her. *She'd see right through me.*

'You've manipulated me.'

'Not at all. The choice is still yours to make.'

'Have I changed so much?' he asked himself, shaking his head slowly. He hesitated briefly. 'Teach me the last lesson.'

'Why?'

He paused. 'I cannot give her what I do not have. I cannot give her hope.'

Kene smiled. 'There was never any mistake. Your faith must be bigger than your fears, my friend. There's no secret word, no charm stone, that is the one simple truth to it.'

Kato wanted to laugh like a mad person. Was *this* the last lesson? He'd expected Kene to add something to him, like putting an egg in an empty basket, and that would be that. It had all come back to him once more. Him, the coward and traitor!

'Yes, indeed,' Kene read his mind. 'It has *always* been about you.'

'Why are you trying to find something in me that is simply not there!' Kato demanded.

'Listen, listen… Listen, my friend,' Kene said tapping him where his heart was. 'Here, and not there.' He gestured with his chin to Kato's head. 'For your mother's sake if nothing else.

'Till today you have acted out of doubt in yourself. Despite your destiny, despite the pathway that brought me to you, the only thing you have is doubt.'

Kato didn't disagree with him. There was no mystery in it; he knew more than anyone what a disappointment he was.

'Please listen Kato,' Kene said sounding desperate. 'Everything depends on it. You,' he spoke slowly and with emphasis, 'will never be able to defeat your fears without faith.'

'I have no faith in myself.'

'I know,' Kene replied. 'I also know there's a reason why the pathway led to you. Did it ever occur to you to leave Apu and run when the leopard opened its maws and snarled at you?' Kato shook his head. He remembered covering his friend to protect him, no matter how useless the gesture was. 'When you chose to save your grandmother and give up your life with me, was it a difficult decision to make?' Kato shook his head again. Kene smiled. 'What will you give in exchange for your mother's life?' Kato stared at him with bloodshot eyes. 'Everything!' he hissed.

'Do you not see, Kato?' Kene looked at him tenderly.

'When you put love first you are brave and courageous. If you have no faith in yourself, start by putting your faith in the people you love.' *It was too simple.* 'Put your faith in them with everything you have, and like a beacon the only place they will lead you to is yourself because that is what love does.'

Kato shut his eyes. He knew it was finally time to face the darkness he'd been running away from his entire life.

'What do I do?' he asked, opening his eyes finally.

'Make your oath to the land. The only way to pass its test is by beating the fear you've carried with you your entire life. Then you will be both a storyteller and free.'

What if I'm still not good enough? The question pried itself into his mind but he dismissed it. There were no two ways about it—he would end his mother's suffering tonight even if it should cost him his life.

'How do I make the oath?'

'You already know how.'

Kato nodded. Kneeling down he grabbed a handful of dirt in his hand.

He stood back up and waited for instructions from Kene.

'It is your oath. You make it. Just address it as the first watcher,' Kene said. 'Oh, and you better be lying down when you eat the earth.'

Kato thought for a while, recalling everything he knew of the oath of his people and nodded.

'Witness my oath, first watcher! I will tell the truth and nothing else. If I break this oath may I and my root be cursed.'

With the oath complete he lay on the ground and shoved the fistful of earth into his mouth. A river of muddy saliva flowed down his throat. Within no time he felt very sleepy and as his mind faded he understood why Kene had advised him to lie down.

Kato groaned with pain as something sharp dug into his back. He felt groggy and found it difficult to focus just yet.

'Never forget that it is in the tribe that you have your identity and your very safety,' a very familiar, deep voice spoke.

His eyes flew open and he found himself looking at a fire-lit earth floor. He suddenly knew where he was even though he couldn't understand how. He felt Apu shivering behind him. He was back at the council hall *that* night.

'Now whose idea was it then?'

'It was my idea, sir,' Apu answered.

Kato felt tears well up in his eyes. In his imagination he'd been defeated by this moment countless times before, and there was no reason why it should go any different now. Every time he'd chosen to look away he'd felt himself become smaller and smaller.

Somehow, through some miracle he was here where everything had begun to unravel. Would it be the same this time too? He felt a strange sense of imbalance as though he might separate from his body any time. As though he was not really in control but was simply observing.

'It was my idea,' Apu repeated, this time in a firmer voice. 'Kato refused but I made him come with me.'

Kato's insides twisted itself into a painful knot. It would be so easy, he thought, to not do anything. To let things go as they will. His mind became heavy with passivity and detached ennui.

No! A voice barged into his quickly dissipating consciousness. *Put your faith in the people you love.* It was Kene.

Like someone being woken from a deep sleep, he felt annoyance at first. *Put your faith in the people you love.* The voice insisted again. He shook his head weakly.

For her sake!

His eyes flew open. *For her sake.* He remembered his purpose.

He glanced back at Apu. The fire glimmered in his thin friend's eyes. He remembered the distant look on his face from that night and his heart squeezed painfully in his chest. Countless times before, he'd weighed himself against the inevitability of this moment: Holding his aching desire for things to go different against the overwhelming strength of his fear. So many times had he thought of this moment that it had come to feel like a real place, as though he were standing at a cross-road. It reminded him of the place in his nightmares that didn't change. The thought sent a loud gong ringing in his mind. In what felt like the moment a cloth is lifted from one's eyes, Kato understood the heart of the matter. They were the same place!

It wasn't just about the moment in the council hall, but every moment that had come before it. While he might have betrayed Apu in that moment he'd been betraying himself his whole life. *It has always been about you.* He recalled Kene's words, and this time he understood the whole of it. Resoluteness took root in him then.

'Kato!' the chief commanded, 'look at me.' He lifted his head and met the chief's eyes. 'It was Apu then?'

A sob broke through his chest. *This time would be different.*

If it had always been about him then the choice that Ghonili had spoken about wasn't the choice between having a voice or not, but the choice between hope and despair. He wasn't here just to defeat one moment in time but choose for the entirety of his life. Kato bit into his lips until he tasted blood. His whole body shook. Sniffing snot back he stood up and looked the chief square in the eyes. Taking a deep breath, he held it in his chest for a long time.

He spoke at last. 'A thousand times it was me.' There were no words but shivering grunts. The faces of the men in the council hall looked strangely distant, the firelight dancing on their skin.

'A thousand times it was me!' he shouted this time. He wasn't going to change his mind. Like a fish bone that has finally been dislodged from a throat Kato felt overwhelming relief. He'd chosen hope.

'So be it,' a voice rumbled, sounding satisfied.

The faces of the men and the council hall began to melt like thawing ice. He struggled to maintain his balance. When the room stopped moving he saw that he was in a huge cavern with giant roots crowding its sides. Some reached down from the centre looking like great tree trunks and the ground looked like a giant maze of interweaving knots and entrails. The gigantic space echoed with vastness and a grey light that looked like moonlight lit it. The only sound was the gentle flowing of a river somewhere. He knew that he was underground because the smell of the earth was damp and rich as only freshly dug soil could be.

He was inside the land, in its heart!

Lakhe's roots were also here somewhere. A mighty presence made itself known, and he could tell that he was being watched, though as far as he could see he was alone.

'WATCHER.'

He turned his head trying to locate the source of the sound, but it came from everywhere.

'WATCHER,' it said again. 'THE OATH WILL BE REMEMBERED.'

He couldn't explain how it happened but a beat began within his heart. Where his heartbeat was present and steady, this one was vast yet gentle.

As though it were the echo of something. He doubted that his heart could really contain the actual beat.

He barely had time to complete the thought because he felt a sensation of falling, and before he could react the cavern spun out of sight.

'Kato!' He found Kene shaking him when he came to.

He sat up wiping the taste of earth from his mouth. 'Watcher,' he said. 'It called me watcher.'

Kene knelt down and hugged him tightly. 'You are the storyteller!'

'Yes,' Kato agreed, his heart soaring. 'For the first time I know what hope feels like.'

Kene smiled. 'There has never been a storyteller without hope. A storyteller without hope is like a river without a shore, constantly buffeted by the winds with nowhere to rest. You'd be destroyed by the stories. Hope is where storytellers rest. Hope that despite every painful story you tell the ending will be beautiful.'

'I wasn't ready when you first met me.' He understood now.

'No, you were too focused on your darkness. When I followed the pathway and found a mute child without hope, I had my doubts too. She, on the other hand, never doubted. So ironic, the one who is lost never doubted. Maybe that's what it takes to truly understand hope.' He shook his head, laughing softly.

'What are you talking about?'

'The debt you owe the muza muza,' Kene said.

'I remember. What is it?'

Kene released him awkwardly and stood up. 'I don't know if it will work.' He watched him circling the fire. 'What is it?'

Kene stopped his pacing and stood opposite him with the fire between them. Kato waited for him to continue. 'I think there's a way to help her find her way,' Kene said. 'But I need your help.'

'What do you mean?'

'I've been busy folding the tapestry of our pathway back and there's just one crease left.' He looked as though he was considering something monumental. 'Tonight, we leave.'

Kato felt as though someone had punched him in the gut.

'The muza muza alone will be left behind because it has lost its way,' Kene said softly.

'What will happen to it?' Kato asked.

For a while there was just the sound of the crickets and owls.

'It will forever remain lost,' Kene said looking pained. Kato regarded him for a long time and finally something dawned on him. 'Kene, what is it to you?'

The little giant hesitated. 'The muza muza is Kuthu, she who was made after me. She is my sister.'

'What then do you propose we do?' Kato asked after a while.

'The final crease is where she wandered out of the pathway. You are the storyteller,' Kene explained, 'Maybe if you stand in the gap and tell a story she will find her way home.'

Kato lifted an eyebrow. 'And then what?'

'Then... there's only hope.'

The memory of the strange incident by the riverside came to Kato's mind. 'She came to visit me at the river.'

Kene laughed. 'She's been keeping an eye on you all this time.'

'Let us be off then,' Kato said, standing up. He felt Kene's hand on his wrist and looked down. The little giant was still sitting. 'Are you sure that you have it all?' he said without looking up.

'Have faith in me, my friend,' Kato said smiling.

A weight seemed to leave the little giant. He looked up with a joyful grin.

23

The Debt

Kato followed the little giant, completely befuddled. He'd expected Kene to take him somewhere out to the great forest. Instead, he was leading him to their backyard. He really began to question the whole thing when Kene continued into the hollow where his mother's prolific sow slept with another new litter.

Worn away by the incessant rooting the place stood lower than the adjoining areas, yet it remained unflooded even during peak monsoon because of a small channel his father had dug in it toward the slope. Still, it was always slippery because of the swill and the proclivity of pigs for mud. Kene chose his spot carefully and motioned to him.

Kato went and stood beside him silently. *Maybe none of this is an accident,* he thought. *To think that this place where I lived my whole life is where she lost her way many lifetimes ago.*

'Look closely, Kato,' Kene said. 'This will never be seen here again.'

Reaching a hand into the empty space before him Kene *drew* back the night and it opened onto something that wasn't really there. Kato's mind reeled as it tried to understand what had just happened. The unremarkable space that had always existed in this slippery hollow had just been pushed aside as if it was a shawl and through the crack in the air he saw the impossibly tall Lakhe.

He blinked. *It was really there!*

He tore his eyes away from the impossibility and gaped at Kene. 'How does Lakhe remain hidden from human eyes?' All the talk of *creases* and pathways began to make sense. 'Has this always been here?'

'It has been both always here and not here,' Kene replied. 'When I remove this last crease our pathways will be severed from yours.' Gesturing at a point before the crease, Kato said, 'Stand here.'

Kato obeyed him, but not before peering into the gap first. There stood Lakhe, mountain tall, already looking as if she belonged to another world. On her branches many ape-like shapes frolicked like happy ferrets, and there on the boulder that he knew well were seated several child-like beings with the grace of feline kings. Others that were unfamiliar to him sauntered amongst the vegetation. 'Are they also all leaving?' he asked sadly.

'Some. These mountains will still have some charm, but much less than before.'

'What do I do?'

'Tell a story my friend.' Kene smiled at him.

'Any story?'

'No, tonight we'll need a story that can show a lost spirit its way home. Tell a story that truly means something to you.'

'How do I know that it's done?'

'You'll know, my friend.'

Kato took several deep breaths and closed his eyes. *A story that truly means something to me.* The first story his mother ever told him.

'Once there was Alhou, the creator who existed since the beginning. He made men and the spirits, the animals, the trees and the plants, the rivers and the mountains: everything that is. But before he made men he said to himself, "Man will be weak—fragile as a dead leaf and as foolish as a newly hatched chick. On his own he will not survive this place that I've created." So he decided to make other beings before man, wiser, stronger and much longer-lived. These spirits went where their people went, guiding them and teaching them. Then, there were the *old ones* who were made to watch over the land. They were the first storytellers.'

He opened his eyes halfway through the story and found Kene scanning the darkness. Being very careful to not let the story drop he closed his eyes once more and continued. When he finished, he began all over again as Kene had asked him to. He neither felt nor heard anything for a while but on the third retelling he heard Kene excitedly whisper, '*She's here!*'

Kato kept the story going but opened his eyes. The same spiralling dust and leaves had appeared by his home.

It wandered towards the woodpile first, its frantic movements suggesting hesitation and doubt. The story continued—louder now. She moved over to his mother's garden before quickly whirring up to their gazing bench. There was a loud *whoosh* as she whirled around angrily, sending leaves and twigs scattering everywhere. The frustration was growing rapidly.

She knows. Kato thought. It was evident that there was very real urgency in its movements. She knows that she will be left behind. He heard what sounded like a muffled howl and then a sob.

Kato watched it repeating the same zig-zag pattern for a while, the urgency of its movements suggesting its increasing distress. He felt overwhelming sympathy; it reminded him of himself. He changed the story. 'Once upon a time there was a boy named Kato. He was born a mute and ran from all his fears. There were those who loved him but his heart was so closed that all he saw was despair and defeat...' He told the story of his own darkness.

For some reason the muza muza had been behaving as though it were blind until now. Even under the waning moon Kato could see it but it appeared as though there was a cloak hiding him and Kene from her. However, now that Kato's story gathered strength she stopped buzzing about and stood still for a while before suddenly heading in their direction. He heard Kene inhale audibly. Within no time the spiralling dome was buzzing less than a couple of footsteps away. Kato felt lightheaded with happiness. The accompanying beat within his heart began to reverberate through his chest making his ribcage tremble.

She appeared to have met another obstacle, like a river that has been diverted. No matter how much she tried she failed to join Kene. Again and again she hurled herself towards them but like an insect caught in a torrent it failed to clear the force that kept it away. The sobbing was now clearly audible. It sounded terribly sad and terrified.

The more he told the story the clearer his vision became, and he began seeing *pathways* with his own eyes. The path leading to the crease ran diagonal to the pathway that the spirit was obsessively buzzing around in, and somehow despite how close it came it simply failed to cross over. The whole thing reminded him of dung beetles that village children would tie with strings and play with. No matter how freely they seemed to buzz around, their freedom extended only to the length of their string.

Kato felt a deep wellspring of tenderness in his soul. *So close to being forever lost, so close to finding its way home.* He wished that his story could become *its* story too and without any conscious thought he began to tell *their* story. He told of a life spent running, of hope awakened and then lost, of betrayal and disappointments: Of a world that was being forever changed, of hope awakened and faith in a brand-new day. He lost himself in his story and when he opened his eyes, he saw the muza muza staring right at him. There was no more dust and leaves but a young girl with wild hair and a lost look. She had very long hair that covered the gaunt body to her knees and on her face was written a thousand sad stories. She shifted restlessly, her eyes pleading for help. He felt Kene's hands take his.

She stood just outside the pathway that connected Kene and the crease where Lakhe waited. He saw her helplessness and the pleading in her eyes. He remembered the gaunt hand that had taken the charm stone from him.

Acting purely on instinct he took his shawl and used it to join the spirit's pathway to the one that led into the crease. Laid lengthwise between the two paths it looked like the crimson line in the shawl was a third pathway that connected them. The story continued unbroken. The spirit seemed to hesitate for a second and then leapt over the shawl into the crease! Kene's hand left his in an instant and he watched with fascination as his friend half flew and caught the muza muza around the waist.

'Sister!' he exclaimed sharply, the strain of his powerful emotions twisting his voice. The spirit struggled to get away but relented when Kene whispered into her ear, 'You're home.' Kato heard the whisper. Slowly Kene guided the muza muza into the gap. Kato smiled, seemingly forgotten by Kene. His heart overflowed as he watched her scamper up the gentle slope to Lakhe.

'Thank you,' Kene said from inside the gap. 'You are a storyteller like none before. No other storyteller has ever bridged pathways.'

Kato beamed with pride.

'What would have happened if I did not owe her a debt? Would she have continued to be lost?'

'Would you have refused to help?'

He shook his head and smiled. 'We've all been manipulated.'

'I suppose it's time then?'

'Remember my stories, Kato.' Kene waved, his face a mix of both melancholy and joy. His voice sounded as though it was coming from a chasm deep underground and not a few arms' length away. 'The world *is* changing, but you must not waver in your task.'

'I will remember everything you taught me, my friend.'

Kato quickly rolled up his shawl and threw it into the gap. Kene caught it with remarkable quickness. 'You won't have another like it.' It was spoken as a fact. Kato nodded. He no longer needed a line on a shawl to show him his anguagha.

'Now you'll know what it is like to have a grandmother.'

The little giant gave him a warm smile. 'Until the moon touches your mountain's peak,' Kene said.

What did he mean?

'When I fold away the last crease in our pathway, it will send a wave through all other pathways. The anchor your mother's spirit is using to stay in your world will come loose and she will leave you for good … I'm sorry my friend, it is the way it must be.'

Kato stood silently, a giant rock wedged in his chest. His heart forgot to beat for the longest time and his ears began pounding with its own rhythm. He'd known that the moment of the final farewell was coming. Yet, to be told in no uncertain terms and with such finality was mind shattering.

He nodded tearfully.

'She isn't the mother you knew, Kato. She's been half of the other world since she came back to you. They don't need words there.'

He understood what Kene meant.

'Make it count.' Kene repeated once more.

Glancing up at the descending moon first Kato gave Kene a long final look. 'Goodbye my friend.' The last thing he saw as he turned away was Kene bowing deeply with his grandmother's shawl in his little hands.

Exhaustion suddenly hit him and he crawled out of the ditch on all fours as he'd done at the wreckage. Huffing for breath he slowly climbed to his feet and started walking towards the home where his dying mother waited.

She looked so young. It was as though the magic of the night had turned her into a little girl and he wasn't quite sure whether this was really his mother or she'd switched pathways with Kuthu. He opened the window and watched the moon drift closer to the peak. There was so very little time, yet he hesitated.

As quietly as he could manage, he walked to the bed and sat by her. It took all the strength he had to not simply wrap her in the tightest embrace, but he wanted to watch her undisturbed for a while longer. He noticed the dampness on her forehead and gently wiped it away with one finger. *How frail she's become,* he thought as he watched her chest rise and fall almost imperceptibly. He felt like he was going to unravel at any moment, his grief already threatening to swallow him. But this was for her sake, and he needed to be strong.

He remembered the night he'd run away from her, his heart wounded and bitter. He promised himself that tonight would be different. More than anything in the world, tonight he wanted to send her away with peace.

Making sure that he'd wiped every trace of the tears from his face, he bent and kissed her on her forehead. Iza. He spoke in his heart. Her eyes flew open immediately, as though she'd been waiting for this moment all her life.

She smiled tenderly and struggled to get on her elbows. He quickly bent to help her sit up and wrapped her thin body in his arms. She clung to him like a child. Glancing out the window he saw the moon moving closer to the peak. Afraid that he'd fall apart he hid his face in her hair. It smelled like her sweat, and when he pulled away at last he left a damp spot on her hair.

She turned his face towards her and looked at him closely. He smiled and took her hand. Raising it to his face he let it stay there for a while. She caressed his skin tenderly. All his life he'd wished that he could speak so that he could tell her he loved her. Like the other kids. But he realized now that between them there'd never been any need for words.

He kissed the palm of his right hand and pressed it to her heart. *I love you*. She did the same and he held her hand over his heart. He'd promised himself that he'd be strong for her sake but he'd already begun to unravel. A sob escaped his lips.

Tilting her head she regarded him curiously. Her gaze was shockingly perceptive. She looked like a crane, and Kato understood why Kene said that she was already half of the other world. There was something unearthly about the way she seemed to be looking at his soul rather than his face. She was the same mother he'd always known, yet she was also changed.

'Will you be okay, ilomi?' They were the first words that had passed between them the whole time.

He nodded slowly. His eyes did not waver.

She continued to regard him for a moment longer and then like the sun peeking out from the clouds tenderness replaced the incisive gaze. She smiled, disbelief and pride making her pale cheeks flush warmly like their old self once more.

'You've changed,' she whispered. He leaned in and hugged her once more.

'I was afraid for you, my love,' she murmured, planting a long, warm kiss on the nape of his neck.

He looked out at the moon urgently and now there was but a string's gap between it and the peak. He'd been fighting the panic somehow but now he found himself losing the battle. The final farewell was almost here.

'My strength wanes, ilomi.' She sighed. He understood what was happening. The tears he'd been fighting to keep at bay came on with a vengeance.

Supporting her back with one arm he gently laid her down on the bed. He lay down beside her and pressed his face to hers, their tears converging where their cheeks met. A familiar feeling of sleepiness began to spread over him.

I love you, Iza, he whispered but there was simply a sob, and then silence. The sleep came like the weight of a mountain. 'I love you forever, my heart,' he heard her say just as the last dregs of his conscious mind slipped away.

He woke to find his grandmother shaking him. 'Kato, wake up.' The blurry shape of his mother lay beside him. It seemed like a distant memory, him clambering up beside her, bone weary and heart aching. Immediately aware of his filthy state he hurriedly alighted. 'It's okay. little squirrel.' He felt her hand on his back, tender and comforting. His father was sobbing by his mother's head. 'Ilomi, Ilomi,' he said over and over again. Suddenly aware that something wasn't adding up, his eyes darted to her face and it felt as though his heart had caved in. Sometime during the night, as he lay sleeping beside her, his mother had gone to his grandfather's hunting grounds.

He found her hand through blurry eyes. It still felt warm. So much had happened within the span of a single day and night. He'd discovered hope, become a storyteller at last, saved a lost spirit and said farewell to a little giant who'd taught him how to be storyteller. So much had happened and yet, this moment outweighed them all. He looked at her face that would never smile for him again, eyes that would never light up for him again. He was a storyteller and he knew how to keep her alive in his stories but he knew just as well that she would never hold him as long as he lived.

A sudden memory came to him unbidden. *His mother standing with one hand shading her eyes in the field, watching him walk under the bright sunlight down the slope to her. The wind blew her hair around her face and she called his name again and again...*

When it finally came his sorrow sounded like the cries of a broken animal.

People had begun to gather, and Kato could hear his father sobbing inside. Soon the women would chase everyone else out and start preparing her body for burial. Alone, he held his knees tightly on the bench and rocked back and forth. The grief weighed him down so heavily that almost unconsciously he lowered himself to the cold, hard earth, where his sorrow felt at home.

His grandmother became her old self again, released from the spell of dreadful waiting. She quickly went about organizing everything, sending people to inform the villagers and the chief, supervising the digging of the grave and the slaughtering of a pig for the mourners who would begin coming shortly.

The mourners, as per their usual practice, began to howl and wail, and they took turns to carry this on till the time of the burial. Inside, the womenfolk prepared Nisheli's body for her last journey, washing and combing her long, ebony hair, draping her in her favorite hekimini. Her bead and shell ornaments, however would be removed and stored away for they were inheritances, to be passed down.

Before long he saw Apu and his parents. Apu looked very agitated and kept circling the house, not going in, perhaps afraid of how Kato might react on seeing him. *How terribly I've treated him*, Kato thought sadly. He cupped his hands together and blew into them. '*Whoo, whoo.*' He saw Apu whirl around and frantically try to locate the sound. He started walking away from his house, heading towards the communal granaries.

'*Whoo, whoo*', a similar call came back this time. Apu was following.

He stood waiting behind the granaries. A '*whoo, whoo*' came again and he responded. Apu finally came into view, breathless and bowed over. 'How you made me search for you, you ape!' he exclaimed. The words meant more to him than anything else in that moment, much more than a pat on the back and a kind word from anyone else. *He'd been searching for him. He'd found him.*

Overwhelmed with gratitude, he couldn't bring himself to look at Apu and dropped to his knees. Kneeling in front of this friend who was more than a brother he bowed his head and remained there, not bothering to hide the sobs that shook his whole body. He was so terribly tired, and he was glad that there was no more running to do. Apu placed his hands on Kato's shoulder and spoke with compassion through his own tears, 'Whatever it was that made you act like a fool, you can tell me another time. Today, just know that I am very sorry that your kind mother is no more.'

After a long comfortable silence, Apu pointed out an eagle as it flew into the sun's glow, 'Ishou, there she flies!' The souls of good people were said to fly to the land of the dead, beyond Mount Makhel, taking the form of eagles. Kato looked for a long time until his eyes could stand the glare no more, and with a smile he stood up and offered his hand to his friend. They walked back to the mourning and wailing, Apu's hands on Kato's shoulder, just the way it had always been.

The preparation for the burial had taken half the day. Kato was finally allowed to sit by her when the womenfolk deemed her body ready to be presented. With his father and his grandmother beside him he stroked her face and tried his hardest to burn every crease, every curve, every nook, every swell and every hollow on her face, onto his memory. He wanted to remember only the beautiful, healthy woman, the woman who'd been his angel of radiance. But this too was her.

They came and said their farewells one after the other. '...*go well,*' they'd say, and '*forgive us if we've wronged you.*' Kato listened to them coming and going—the grief blurring his eyes so that they all appeared faceless—each asking for her grace, each reminiscing some shared memory with her, each sending her off on her long flight. *He* did not want to ask for her forgiveness, did not want to send her off, did not want to reminisce. She was his mother, he her son, and until today she'd been everything to him. There was nothing more to it, nothing would ever change it.

He felt his father's hand on his arm and looked up. It was his uncle and aunt. His eyes did not waver as he watched them walk up to his mother's body. He was not afraid any longer.

'Go well, Nisheli,' his uncle said, unexpectedly gentle. 'Your kindness will not be forgotten.' They stood there wordlessly. 'Forgive us...' his uncle said at last with a knot in his voice. It sounded as though there was more to come but only silence followed.

Ignoring his wife's hand that sought to take him away, he gave Kato a long look. There were no words but he read the eyes and smiled. His uncle nodded and let himself be led away.

The carriers finally put her body on a stretcher and the procession headed for the burial grounds. A boy's entire lifespan played in his mind as he followed behind with his grandmother and father, a lifespan of her constant presence. Unbearable anguish clawed furrows into his soul. *We'll leave her behind.* Even though he was holding up better than he'd ever hoped the thought made him go blind with grief. He stumbled but felt a hand quickly steady him.

'Careful, ishou!' It was Apu. He'd found him again.

He saw the hole they'd dug for her. It was in a place where both sunlight and rain would fall unbothered. They silently gathered around the grave and stood for a while. He desperately looked at her face, trying to commit every feature into his mind. *This too is her.*

When they began to lower her body into the earth, it was his grandmother who broke first. 'My child! My child!' she wailed as she beat her chest. One of her friends quickly caught her before she fainted and fell to the ground, and the womenfolk immediately gathered around to massage her limbs.

We'll leave her here, alone...

The villagers froze, heads turned frantically trying to locate a keening sound unlike anything they'd ever heard before. The embodiment of Kato's grief had taken the form of a guttural wail, and this time there was no shame or secrecy to it. Iza, Iza, Iza! He screamed, and it did not matter to him that it was undecipherable, did not care that they stared at him, shocked by the guttural screaming. He would have this, and no one was going to stop him.

Like ants following a secret language they found their way to each other: his father, his grandmother and him. In that moment, standing on freshly dug soil that would soon cover her, they became removed from everyone else in their particular sorrow that they alone shared.

It was done. Nisheli had been laid into her grave and covered with the earth. It would take months and years for Kato to not expect to hear her voice from the kitchen when he woke up in the morning, a lifetime to not miss her when he heard one of her stories from someone else, and more than a lifetime to forget the way she stood waiting for him in the field, the sun in her hair and longing in his heart. His mother was gone, like the April wind, like the August rain, like the harvest in October, gone but not really. Her stories lived in him, along with Kene's too.

24

Aniqhi Once More

Lhokashe felt every bit of the fifty-five years, each year seemingly pushing his head down lower and lower, until his chin was resting on his chest. It had been two months since he'd laid Nisheli into her grave, two months he couldn't believe he'd gotten through. Like a newborn learning to walk, he'd had to focus all his strength on simply taking one step after another.

If only I had called her name more, if only I had spent more mornings like this with her, if only I had been a man with more words, if only… How was he to live knowing that he could have done so much more? It tore him into a thousand small pieces to live with the knowledge of his deficiencies in loving her, and now it was far too late.

Khuzheli looked at the drooping figure of her son-in-law from the doorway and sighed. 'The poor dear,' she thought to herself. It was no easy matter for a mother to bury her own daughter in her old age, but Lhokashe seemed to have lost the will to live after losing Nisheli. She understood both his anguish and his befuddlement. Her daughter truly had been the voice for three people, and now that she was gone the survivors were as lost as nestlings without the mother. *But how long?* she thought. Kato needed his father. She'd stayed on for good after Nisheli's passing and did the best she could for her grandson, but a boy needed his parent. Perhaps it was time to have a second talk with her son-in-law, even though the first one had failed completely. So lost was she in her thoughts that she didn't hear Kato sneaking up behind her.

'O, shalapa!' she exclaimed in terror when he suddenly grabbed her by the shoulders. 'You scared me, you naughty boy!' she shouted and the two of them began to laugh uncontrollably until they were wheezing for breath.

Lhokashe was drawn back into the sunlight from the dim recesses of his regrets by the sound of boisterous laughter. The house had been so bereft of anything resembling joy for the last three months that it jolted him like an ant bite, and after months he truly saw his son. He couldn't help but notice that Kato had Nisheli's eyes and her hair too, and the chin and forehead of his father. He was their son! And perhaps as Nisheli would have wanted, that thought drew forth the same keen fierceness that she had once felt. *Yes, it will go well*, he thought as he let their joyful abandon coax a smile out of him.

'Stop that now, little squirrel,' his grandmother begged.

Kato staggered behind his grandmother into the courtyard, trying to put a stop to the unending bout of laughter. Just as it seemed to peter out all it took was one look at each other and then it would begin all over again. They crouched on the ground in the warm sun, massaging their aching bellies. His little puppy climbed on his back and licked his face happily, making Kato laugh even more. It was a present from his grandmother and they were already inseparable.

He looked at his grandmother fondly. She seemed to have aged so much in a matter of a few months and Kato felt ashamed that he'd not noticed before. So much had changed though in these two months.

The war at Kohima had ended and the Japanese army had been defeated. Even though the villagers would still carry on with their lives as before, irrespective of the outcome, there was mourning in some homes. Three boys, including Ato who'd always been kind to Kato, lost their lives in the battle. Only Ato's body could be brought back for burial because bombs had mangled the bodies of the other two. *'Apu! Kato! You better be good!'* were his last words to the boys.

'I'm going to your apuza Ghonili's house later,' his apuza interrupted his thoughts. 'I want to give it a little cleaning. I know it's been months but it just feels bad to have her house fall apart. And she might still return.' Her eyebrows furrowed in an expression of concern.

With the war, his mother's passing, and the return of the boys from the war, no one had noticed that Ghonili had been missing. Initially people assumed that she'd gone on one of her forays into the jungles. But when her house remained unattended for weeks and then a month, questions started.

'Come to think of it,' his grandmother said. 'Wasn't that strange visit to you the last time we saw her?'

Kato squinted. *The night Kene returned.*

'I do think that was the last time anyone saw her!' she exclaimed. 'Where are you, ipami?'

Kato suddenly began laughing his funny laugh. *What was your story, apuza Ghonili?* His eyes twinkled. It made sense now, all the things she knew, the strange meeting. *She'd smelled something on me.* His laughter became even louder. *What was your story?*

His grandmother stared at him with a puzzled look. He stood up, offering a hand to her. He felt sorry for her because if he was right she'd be cleaning an empty house for no reason at all.

=

Aghoto, the teacher, had come back with a completely changed demeanor. Morose and decidedly moody, he presided over the first day of class. 'So tell me then,' he said to a girl, 'how would you send a message to someone who is in another country?' The girl seemed to think for a moment, and replied as though it was the most obvious thing ever, 'Why, you send someone from the village with the message!' Everyone burst out laughing when she next added in a soft voice that grew increasingly more hesitant, 'Though... if it is that far he may never return...'

Like the sun emerging from behind the clouds after a storm, the classroom seemed to regain its old boisterousness again. The teacher too couldn't help himself, and the silliness of it all broke through his melancholy with a vengeance, so that there was finally no sane person left in the classroom.

'Kato, please stay back after the class,' the teacher said while dismissing classes for the day. Kato looked quizzically at Apu and Ilhopu who shrugged their shoulders, 'We'll be by the big tree outside.'

'Come here, Kato,' the teacher motioned for him to come to the front. 'Sit, sit,' he said pointing to the first bench. *He doesn't seem angry, so not something I did*, Kato thought as he sat down. 'I heard about your dear mother.' He leaned forward and placed a hand on his shoulder. 'I'm extremely sorry my boy. She was always kind to me.'

A long silence passed where the teacher seemed to be lost in his thoughts. Just as Kato was wondering whether he'd been dismissed or not, the teacher spoke again, 'It's not as one would expect, the big, wide world.' He smiled a strange smile, part happy and part sad. 'They didn't accept me, I was turned away the minute I got there,' he said, laughing self-deprecatingly as he continued. 'I was too embarrassed to return immediately, so I took temporary employment as a house-servant.'

Kato gaped at him in shock. Aghoto was respected by everyone in the village— he was after all the chosen one whom the white men conferred with—and to think that outside the village he'd had to become someone's servant. *What a strange thing the big, wide world!*

'Why am I telling you all this, you might wonder,' he continued. 'You would be correct to wonder because I do not really know myself, though there was something I did want to tell you about.' He trailed off thoughtfully.

The truth of it was that his experiences in Kohima had shaken Aghoto to his roots; every belief he'd held onto with sureness suddenly seemed to have become indeterminate. What measures he'd previously used to determine his worth and standing in the world had been exposed as being pitifully inadequate. The truth was that he'd felt his roots pulling away, and it had terrified him.

He'd wanted to tell someone about it all, but somehow he'd felt too embarrassed. Kato was the perfect person, because, though not by choice, he could listen but not interrupt, hear but not carry tales. Aghoto realized it then, and he flushed with shame knowing what he was doing, 'Thank you,' he said suddenly, catching Kato completely by surprise. Kato simply shrugged with what he hoped was a neutral expression, not knowing how else to respond.

'Ah! Now I remember!' Aghoto exclaimed. 'I saw a wonderful thing while I was in Kohima!' His sudden fervor caught Kato unawares, but his interest also flared to life. 'I saw a white woman, a blind white woman,' he said, hunching over and using his hands more while he talked. 'She could read!'

Kato was mystified. How could a blind woman read?

'She used a book that had dots on it, not like the books we use,' Aghoto said, pricking tiny imaginary holes into the bench to illustrate what he was talking about. 'Every letter had a certain shape that these dots represented, and the woman had been taught to read by feeling them!'

Kato was amazed! It was as though a door of new possibilities had opened up to him. What had taken root in him when he'd seen the photograph for the first time sprouted in that moment.

'When I saw her, I was immediately reminded of you. I'm sure that out there,' he stretched his arms wide, 'in the big wide world, you will find your voice.'

The events over the last six months had brought a feeling of disquietude to the entire village. No one was sure what was happening. For countless years the land had echoed the same voices again and again, people had lived and died the same again and again, but all of a sudden, the noises had become so much louder and terrifying. The grinding of metal on metal, and the sounds of explosions, had changed the rhythm of the land; it felt like the ground was being pulled from under their feet. But Kato? He wasn't afraid today. In this strange newness, he was sure he would find a way to tell the stories of those within him.

Ba bum! Ba bum! Ba bum! There it was! The heartbeat of the land!

He heard it sometimes, like a comforting reminder. The land remained and it knew him. He told it stories because unlike people it did not need words to understand. Today he felt its joy as his own hope soared. *Faith!*

'Kato,' Aghoto shook him from his thoughts, 'don't be sad. She'll live here.' He placed his hand on his heart. Kato gave him the brightest smile he'd ever seen and nodded his head.

He came out and saw Apu with Narto. The little imp had one hand on the tree and was waving his hands about as he talked, while Narto's laugh tinkled in the open air. *When?* Kato thought as he smiled wryly to himself. Shaking his head, he quietly took the long way back to his home, leaving Apu the first-class romantic descended from the great hero Khaipu to his romance.

It had come full circle. Almost exactly a year ago Kene had come looking for a storyteller, a year ago when winter was still thawing over the land. Now as Kato watched a flock of Amur Falcon flying towards the river Doyang, he remembered afresh the year that had passed. The muza muza, the shi-kheu, the aki-ghau, the ayithu-amiche-kupu-u, Kene; as the smoke of battle had finally begun to clear from the land Kato could sense that the magic of the old ways had receded. Now there were simply little echoes, no doubt with time even those would be completely silenced. The stories are where they would live until the time came again for them to awaken. Kato felt the urgency, the fullness of the stories within him raring to be let free.

He was almost there. Towards the top, just before he crested the hill there was the sky and nothing beyond, and the familiar sight filled his heart with longing. A year ago he'd have heard them long before he was able to look down at them, their pentatonic singing filling him up with joy—*hoi, hoi, hoi*. But that was a year ago; today there stood his father, alone. As he began the walk down he could almost make himself believe that he saw her standing there through his tears—*the wind in her hair, and longing in his heart*. A lifetime to forget her, more than a lifetime…Wiping the wetness from his eyes he began to walk faster. They were going to reclaim their field from the ugly, soot blackened wreck. He began running as he'd once done with his arms outstretched and a smile broke on his face.

Epilogue

The rumbling and clattering was so loud that Kato couldn't hear what the man beside him was saying. 'Will take another day!' the man shouted to be heard above the noise. Kato winced and nodded his head. The man quickly led him out of the printing floor and ushered him into his office.

'It is quite loud,' he said sinking into his chair. 'Please sit, Mr Kato.' Kato took a seat gratefully. He wrote something in his diary and passed it to the publisher.

'Oh yes! I totally forgot!' Mr Dey said reaching into his drawer and pulling out a book. 'The first copy!' Kato took it with a smile. *The Old Ones*, it said on the cover in beautiful, bold cursive. *I wish you could see me, Kene*, he thought. With a satisfied nod he rose and shook the man's hand and walked out onto the very busy streets of Kohima.

It was 1964, exactly twenty years after the battle of Kohima. There were many people from outside who were visiting, and Kohima was more crowded than it had been in a long time. The 20th anniversary was a big affair and along with tourists and government officials there were both Britishers and Japanese who'd come to pay homage to their fallen comrades.

Kato sat in a small teashop opposite the Kohima War cemetery. The first page of the book was open, and he was thinking about what he was to write on it. 'Chaha,' the errand boy said, depositing the teacup hastily, spilling a little tea on the table. 'You little rascal, can't you do anything properly?' the owner scolded the boy while apologetically wiping the tea from the table. Kato smiled at her and was reminded of a time when he and Apu were just as rascally as the boy. He suddenly knew what he would write and bent with pen.

To,
My giant Apu,
The fields of our boyhood are blooming again. Let's go back to visit together.
Kato

He looked at it again and closed the book with a smile. Apu had married Narto and lived in Dimapur with their three kids. He worked as a surveyor in the land revenue department, and with Kato being just as busy in his work as a librarian in the state library they could hardly ever meet. He was still unmarried at thirty-three, much to the frustration of his father who still lived in the village. His grandmother had passed on two years ago and he regretted not being able to finish the book before her passing, but he was happy knowing that she was with her daughter and husband in their hunting grounds.

'Can I have a cup of tea please?' a man with a strange accent said in English. Kato looked up and saw a tall, lean man in his mid-forties. The man smiled at him and sat on the same bench. He felt a very vague sense of recognition. He quickly rapped a knuckle on the narrow table and indicated that the gentleman wanted a cup too.

'Hello, my name is Hashimoto Kenji,' he said and extended a hand. Kato shook his hand, nodded, wrote on his diary and passed it to him.

'Ah!' the man said apologetically. 'Excuse my rudeness.' Kato waved a hand dismissing the need for any apologies. He wrote something else and passed it to Hashimoto again. 'Oh yes, I fought in the war. I was taken prisoner in the battle here at Kohima. I've returned to pay my respects to my comrades, and also, to be frank, I thought of these mountains,' he said with a mysterious twinkle in his eyes.

'So, what do you do then?' Hashimoto asked.

'A storyteller!' he exclaimed looking at the diary again. 'How wonderful!' Leaning in conspiratorially he whispered to Kato, 'Don't think me crazy but would you like to hear the story of how I met a spirit in your mountains twenty years ago?' Kato gave him an enthusiastic nod. Hashimoto began his story, 'I was with my men on the way to Kohima…' Kato's smile grew wider and wider as the story went on.

GLOSSARY

Achepho	Fermented bamboo shoot
Aizei	An often-used expression translating to 'O, mother!'
Aliha	A small, stilted hut that is used both as a resting place and temporary storage house in the fields
Apuza	Grandmother
Avi	A semi-feral buffalo of the Gaur family, that has great traditional significance
Dao	A cutting tool that very closely resembles a machete
Hekimini	A wraparound skirt, a type of sarong
Ilomi	A very tender way of calling someone 'my most loved'
Iza	My mother (The general noun for mother is aza)
Jhum cultivation	A style of agriculture that involves setting fire to patches of land. The resulting ash fertilizes the ground but, after a certain period, the land must be allowed to rest since the soil becomes less and less fertile due to runoff during the monsoons. This style of cultivation is far less efficient than terrace cultivation.
Thalaxu	Spider
Timi-ala	Literal translation is 'more-than-man'. Timi is the Sumi universal noun for mankind, and ala simply means more.
Tu-umi	A loose translation is 'witch'; more accurately, shaman

ACKNOWLEDGMENTS

I wish to thank my wife, my parents, my siblings, and my in-laws. *Giants* would not have come about without their unwavering support.

I also wish to thank my agent Kanishka Gupta of Writer's Side, for taking a chance on an absolute unknown. A very big thank you to Aparna Kapur, my editor, for keeping me on my toes and honest!

Furthermore, I wish to make special mention of Late Mr. K. Ghulakha P. Swu of Lazami village. An exceptional storyteller of the Sumi traditions, he gave me a new appreciation for the lore and stories of our forefathers.

I also make special mention of Late Rev. Aheto Sema. This was a man who had a vision that shone like the mid-day sun. His legacy continues in many young women and men.

I also wish to make a disclaimer that *Giants* is purely a work of fiction, and isn't meant to be treated as a serious academic work. Creative liberties have been taken, but I believe that the essence has been treated with respect.

ABOUT THE AUTHOR

In his writings Huthuka Sumi hopes to apprehend the liminal spaces where symbols speak more powerfully than literal words and meanings. Besides writing, Huthuka is a studious nostalgist and will be found scouring the web for things that reek of the 90s. Oh, and he likes building stuff with wood.

HarperCollins *Publishers* India

At HarperCollins India, we believe in telling the best stories and finding the widest readership for our books in every format possible. We started publishing in 1992; a great deal has changed since then, but what has remained constant is the passion with which our authors write their books, the love with which readers receive them, and the sheer joy and excitement that we as publishers feel in being a part of the publishing process.

Over the years, we've had the pleasure of publishing some of the finest writing from the subcontinent and around the world, including several award-winning titles and some of the biggest bestsellers in India's publishing history. But nothing has meant more to us than the fact that millions of people have read the books we published, and that somewhere, a book of ours might have made a difference.

As we look to the future, we go back to that one word—a word which has been a driving force for us all these years.

Read.